WALKING THE
LAKELAND FRINGES
The South-West

Mary Welsh

Published by Sigma Leisure – an imprint of Sigma Press, 1 South Oak Lane, Wilmslow, Cheshire SK9 6AR, England.

British Library Cataloguing in Publication Data
A CIP record for this book is available from the British Library.

ISBN: 1-85058-679-9

Typesetting and Design by: Sigma Press, Wilmslow, Cheshire.

Cover picture, illustrations and maps: Christine Isherwood

Printed by: MFP Design and Print

Disclaimer: the information in this book is given in good faith and is believed to be correct at the time of publication. No responsibility is accepted by either the author or publisher for errors or omissions, or for any loss or injury howsoever caused. Only you can judge your own fitness, competence and experience.

Contents

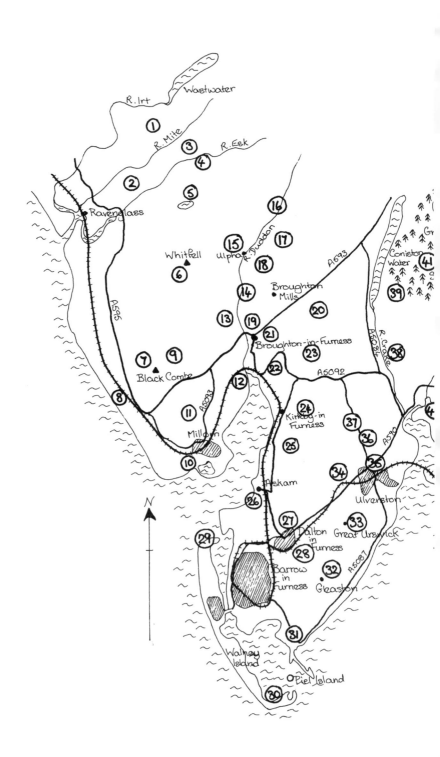

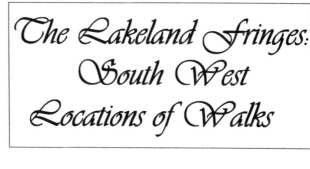

The Lakeland Fringes:
South West
Locations of Walks

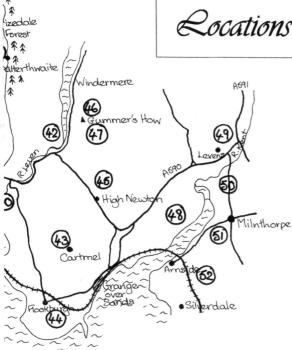

Grizedale Forest

Satterthwaite

Windermere

A591

46 ▲Gummer's How

42 47

49 Levens R. Kent

45

A590

High Newton

50

48

43

Milnthorpe

Cartmel

51

Grange over Sands

Arnside 52

Flookburgh

44

●Silverdale

R. Leven

Walk 1: Irton Pike

Lay-by close to Nether Wasdale – Flass Tarn – Irton Fell – Irton Pike – Stone memorial – London Head – Nether Wasdale

Start/finish: Lay-by on the small triangle formed by the Wasdale, Santon Bridge and Gosforth roads junction, east of Nether Wasdale (GR 129038).

Type of walk: A great 5½-mile walk over rough fell and through delightful woodland. The climb up Irton Fell is quite steep so take your time and pause to enjoy the ever-increasing views. The descent from the Pike and the return to Nether Wasdale, through glorious woodland is all easy and most attractive. Some road walking.

Map: OS Outdoor Leisure 6, The English Lakes – south-west.

Nearest towns: Millom, Whitehaven.

Public transport: None.

Refreshments: Two inns at Nether Wasdale – The Screes and Strands.

Public toilets: None.

Irton Pike is the abrupt end of a long ridge that starts from above the Wastwater Screes. On this pleasing walk to the little summit you are likely to have the fells and woodland all to yourself – other folk hurrying on to the higher tops.

The Walk

From the lay-by cross the road bridge over the River Irt. Take the second signposted footpath on the left, immediately beyond Flass House. Continue ahead through a pleasant area of scattered Scots pine to a gate. Beyond, stroll on to pass Flass Tarn on your right and to walk beside a wall on the left. Go through a stile and walk on, with a fine mix of beech, birch and larch to your right.

At the signpost press on, uphill, until you reach a wide grassy ride. Pause here to enjoy a glimpse of Wastwater and its attendant mountains. Turn left and still with the wall to your left, walk for 50 metres. At the three-armed signpost, take the right fork for Eskdale.

Stride the bridleway through the mixed woodland, heather and pungent bog myrtle to cross two railed areas. Climb the slope to a

Bog Myrtle

gate in the trees and then another onto the open fell. Walk ahead, picking the driest way, and then bear slightly right, across more mire, to join the rocky path. This climbs relentlessly, so choose the easiest way to avoid areas where the path is eroded or wet and continue to the top of the slope.

By the small cairn, 50 metres before the wall ahead that edges Miterdale Forest, turn right. Follow the clear green path across the fell. It keeps parallel with the forest wall but lies 100 metres north of it. Stride the airy fell, with its ex-

tensive views across West Cumbria, towards the woodland ahead. Enter the trees by a stile (do not take the gate and stile nearer the wall on your left), and, beyond, walk a permissive path.

A few metres into the trees a forest ride goes away left. Ignore this but note it for your return. Go ahead through the conifers, avoiding fallen trees and wet areas by using well-trodden diversions.

Suddenly and dramatically, through the trees at the edge of the woodland, you can see the lovely mound of the Pike. Follow the clear path to the summit and stay awhile, lazing on a cushion of heather, to take in the wonderful view. Look towards Wastwater to see Red Pike, Yewbarrow and Kirk Fell to the left of Great Gable. Nearer are Whin Rigg and Illgill Head, both overshadowing the lake.

Return from the top to the ride, now on your right, that you noted when you entered the forest. Bear right and continue downhill to join a wider track. Go on downhill. Watch out for a narrow path that continues to drop down, going off right, This brings you steadily downhill to join a wide forest road. Turn left and walk to a stile beside a double gate to the road. Turn right.

As you go look for the stone memorial in memory of William Malkinson, a Wesleyan local preacher, who died at this place on Sunday, February 21 1886. The large inscription ends: "BE YE ALSO READY".

Walk on to follow the road as it descends through woodland. Where it makes a sharp swing left, take the signposted track on the right. Just before the gate to dwellings named London Head, take the footpath on the right, to go behind the cottages. Join a forest ride and continue on (left). Pass through two gates and continue as directed by the footpath sign through an open area.

Enter a dark plantation where the path underfoot, though not waymarked, is clear, leading you to another open area. Follow the path through the delightful clearing beneath the flaring Shepherd Crags. Then follow the path downhill. A few metres before the ford over Mecklin Beck, take the easy-to-miss footpath on the right (signpost often obscured by vegetation) to climb a stile in the wall to join a forest ride.

Ford the beck on convenient boulders and, a few metres on, take a waymarked narrow footpath dropping down left. Follow it as it swings right and continues along the edge of a young plantation under the magnificent slopes of Latterbarrow. Watch out for the stile on the left, where two walls come together.

Beyond the stile, stroll diagonally across the large pasture to a gate in the bottom right corner. Continue in the same direction to a ladder stile to the road. Turn right to walk the road over the Irt and regain the start of the walk.

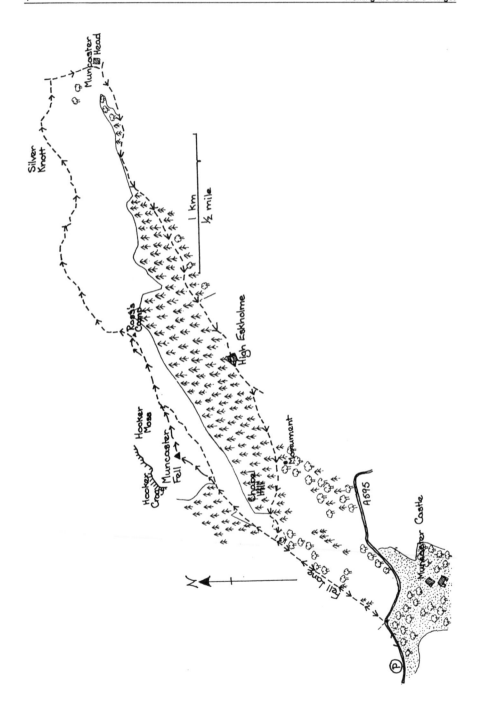

Walk 2: Muncaster Fell

Muncaster car park – Fell Lane – Hooker Crag – Muncaster Fell – Ross's Camp – Muncaster Head farm- High Eskholme – Chapel Hill – Fell Lane – Car park

Start/finish: The large car park on the A595, opposite the main entrance to Muncaster Castle (GR 098966).

Type of walk: This 7-miler includes pleasing walking along a fine ridge. You return through the valley bottom, finishing with a steepish climb through shady woodland along a good track.

Map: OS Outdoor Leisure 6 (new series).

Nearest towns: Millom, Whitehaven.

Public transport: Stagecoach Cumberland from Whitehaven – alight after Muncaster Mill, at right turn for Ravenglass, inquiries 01946 63222. The car park start of the walk is 650 metres along the A-road. There are also several community buses. Cumbria Journey Planner inquiries, tel: 01228 606000.

Refreshments: Cafe in Muncaster Castle. Pay your entrance fee at kiosk across from car park.

Toilets: None on walk

Walk left out of the car park and go on along the A-road to where it turns sharp right. Stride ahead on the continuing public bridleway, directing you towards "Eskdale and Hardknott". The excellent tree-lined gated track, named Fell Lane on the OS map, climbs steadily for three quarters of a mile. It then descends a little to a depression edged with rhododendrons.

Go past a three-armed signpost and through a gate to continue on a track that keeps parallel with a large plantation of mixed conifers to your left. Where the forest ends, go ahead on a peaty path that climbs steadily to the trig point on Hooker Crag (757ft/231m). Pause here and enjoy the spectacular view of Lakeland's high fells.

Descend from the summit and follow the green path that continues across a miry area. In summer this is covered with white-topped cotton grass and is most attractive. In winter, the path may be under water and you will have to skirt left of the boggy area to rejoin the path on the far side.

Go on, with patches of mire to either side of the path, to the brow of the next hill, where another incredible view awaits. Descend the clear path for a short distance and pause to look left to see Irton Pike (Walk 1) and lonely Miterdale. To your right lies Eskdale. Then walk right along a narrow path through the bracken to what at first sight looks like a Neolithic remnant. On the granite tabletop is carved Ross's camp, 1883. How did the members of a Victorian shooting party raise the slab into place so that it could be used for their lunches?

Go forward, downhill and bearing left, to a gateless gap in a wall corner. Stroll downhill, using the narrow path beside the wall on your left. Just before the wall juts right for a metre, take a narrow path right that takes you down to a peaty cart track. Follow this (left) as it swings away from the wall to wind across flat ground to come to the start of a delightful grassy trod, well buttressed with granite boulders.

This embanked path climbs a little as it winds round Silver Knott and then descends steadily through heather and lush vegetation to a kissing gate. Walk on to come to a wall. Bear right to climb a stile by a three-armed signpost. Walk ahead down the farm track to Muncaster Head. Turn right before the outbuildings and continue to another cart track, where you turn right again.

Stride the good track, ignoring the stile on the left. Continue on the glorious way, passing through the quiet vale, with deciduous woodland sloping steeply upwards on your right. The track moves into forest, with towering rhododendrons darkening the way. Then the trees cease on the left and open pasture stretches away across the valley bottom. After 1½ miles go through the gate to join a metalled road to pass Yew Tree Cottage and High Eskholme.

Walk on. Take notice of the signboard and keep to the main track for Muncaster Fell. At the next signboard take the right fork to begin a steep climb through deciduous woodland and go on up for just under ½ mile. Here, by a group of cottages away to your left, notice a spectacular monument. This was built in the 19th century to mark the place where, in 1461, Henry VI was found wandering the slopes by shepherds, after the battle of Towton.

Go on up the track to pass through more lush vegetation and burgeoning trees to pass through a gate. Go ahead to pass beneath an arch of rhododendrons to come to Fell Lane and the signpost passed early on your outward journey. Turn left.

Continue down Fell Lane to the A-road and then go on ahead to the place from which you set off.

Ross's Camp

Walk 3: Blea Tarn, Eskdale

Forge Bridge – Milkingstead Bridge – Fell End – Sineytarn Moss – Siney Tarn – Blea Tarn – Hollinghead Bank – River Esk – Milkingstead – Forge Bridge

Start/finish: A wide lay-by west of Forge Bridge (GR 147995) over the River Esk. This can be reached by taking the narrow fell road over Birker Moor; or you can leave the A595 at Gosforth, or Holmrook or from south-east of Muncaster Bridge.

Type of walk: A great 5½-miler that takes you on a good track beside the River Esk. The paths up onto Fell End are well graded and when you reach the old peat gatherers' and miners' track, which lead down to Eskdale, you will find it difficult to believe that you have climbed so high so easily. The route is waymarked, with just a little care required as you find your way round Sineytarn Moss and Siney Tarn. A glorious walk for all the family which you may wish to combine with walk 4.

Map: OS Outdoor Leisure 6 The English Lakes, south west.

Nearest towns: Whitehaven, Millom and Broughton-in-Furness.

Public transport: Nearest station for North Western Trains is Ravenglass, inquiries 0345 484950. From here take the Ravenglass and Eskdale railway (Ratty) (inquiries 01229 717171) to Eskdale Green and walk south to Forge Bridge.

Refreshments/toilets: Dalegarth Station, half a mile further on from the old school.

Cross the road from the lay-by and take the bridleway, signposted Stanley Ghyll, Boot and Upper Eskdale. Stroll through the pleasing woodland, with the River Esk swirling away to your left. Emerge from the trees and enjoy the dramatic view of the mountains at the head of Eskdale. Pass Milkingstead farm away to your right and then take the fine suspension footbridge over the river.

Walk ahead over a pasture to a gate to the road. Cross and continue ahead up the access track to Fisher Ground. Follow the waymarks directing you right and then left to pass between the buildings to a gate into a walled track.

This leads to the narrow gauge railway track, which you should approach and cross with care. Climb the stile opposite to follow a delightful path that at first bears left, with the railway also to your left. Then the path climbs gently through scattered birch and gorse and you emerge from this pleasing quiet corner by a stone-step stile onto open fell.

Stroll on to a crossroads of paths. Go straight ahead to pass through a wall gap to walk beside, on your left, mixed woodland with some very tall Scots pine. Pause here to look back for a delectable view of Harter Fell and Green Crag. At the wall corner, do not pass through the gate but turn sharp right to walk beside the wall on your left. This lovely path passes below the huge outcrops on the north side of Fell End. Look left for glimpses of Miterdale and of Great Bank standing triumphant above the vast plantation of conifers of Miterdale forest.

Stride on, with steep shattered rock slopes to your right and a plantation of sitka spruce, over the wall, on your left. Look back occasionally to see the golden sands around Ravenglass. Then at the brow you can look down, right, into Eskdale and away to the left sprawls the bleak slopes of Illgill Head.

The path brings you to a stile over a fence. Beyond, walk ahead to follow a

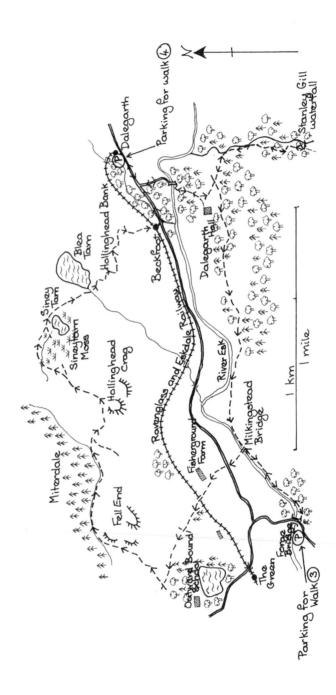

green track that gradually bears right to come beside a wall. Go on, with the wall to your right. Ignore the ladder stile and, at the edge of Sineytarn Moss, look for the path bearing left – it has a cairn at its start.

Go with the path, along the edge of low outcrops, as it winds its way around this very wet area. At another cairn follow the path right, circling an outcrop before it swings left again to go round more mire. Cross a small stream on a railway sleeper and then bear steadily right. The path brings you beside the open water of Siney Tarn, on your right.

The word sine is Old Norse and means to drain. The small stretch of water sits on the end of high ground and is gradually being colonised by invasive reeds. In summer it is the haunt of black headed gulls who are very protective of their young and their territory – be warned.

Carry on along the narrow path to come to the south-west end of charming Blea Tarn. Low heather outcrops enclose this lonely pool on three sides, with Bleatarn Hill reflected in its clear water. Sit beside the tarn – perhaps your lunch stop – and enjoy its isolation, peace and solitude.

Continue along the side of the tarn to join the grand grassy track that zigzags down the steep slopes of Hollinghead Bank. Look for the mine adits and spoil heaps as you descend and remember the miners and peat gatherers who regularly ascended and descended this way.

The track brings you to Beckfoot, where you cross the Ravenglass and Eskdale railway again. Join the Eskdale Road and turn left to walk for 200 metres. Opposite the outdoor centre, once the old school, turn right. Pass the war memorial and continue over the River Esk. Stride on beyond the car park on the left and then Dalegarth Hall, with its round chimneys, on your right. Go through a gate and walk on to a signposted bridleway.

If you wish to combine this walk with walk 4 so that you can visit Stanley Force, stroll on to the gate on the left, signposted "Waterfall".

To continue the walk, turn right to take the stiled and gated bridleway, signposted Eskdale Green. Saunter along the track to a gate into magnificent woodland. Ignore all right and left turns, and go on and on, with no instructions needed. This route, sometimes beside the Esk and sometimes over grassy slopes, is a joy to walk. Eventually it passes Milkingstead footbridge and then the farm. Keep on your outward route to return to Forge Bridge.

Milkingstead Bridge

Walk 4: Stanley Force

Dalegarth Station, Eskdale – Stanley Ghyll – Stanley Force – Dalegarth

Start/finish: Dalegarth Station or its car park (GR 174007). This is the terminus for the Ravenglass and Eskdale Railway, known affectionately as "t' laal Ratty". You may wish to travel the 7 glorious miles, on England's oldest narrow gauge railway, from the station at Ravenglass, or drive through the valley and use the pay-and-display car park.

Type of walk: This short walk of two miles is a delight all the way. Eskdale, one of the few dales without a lake, is a joy to wander, whether you climb the fells, explore the woodlands or visit its many spectacular waterfalls. The walk starts along a quiet lane and then ascends the stepped way to see what is often described as "Lakeland's loveliest waterfall". Much work has been done on the stone steps and the bridges but care is needed as you go deeper in the gill and children should be under firm control. The final stone staircase to see the fall in all its splendour is only for those without vertigo. Wooden steps from the second footbridge take you up the opposite side of the rocky gorge, but if you go on beyond these to the very top of the gill and the cliff edge, take extreme care. This walk is pleasantly combined with walk 3.

Map: OS Outdoor Leisure 6 The English Lakes, south west.

Nearest towns: Whitehaven, Millom, Broughton-in-Furness

Public transport: Ravenglass is on the A595 coast road between Broughton and Whitehaven, but there are no Stagecoach Cumberland buses along this road. North Western Trains run along the Lancaster – Barrow – Ravenglass – Carlisle line, inquiries 0345 484950. These connect with the "Ratty" line, inquiries 01229 717171.

Refreshments/toilets: Ravenglass and Dalegarth Station.

Turn right out of the car park, or the tiny station, and walk the walled road (which can be busy in summer) for 300 metres. Turn left opposite the old school, now an outdoor centre. Walk the lane, which is lined with fine trees. Cross the River Esk by a stone bridge. Peep over the parapet to see the very deep dark-blue water channelled between bleached rocks.

Carry on along the lane where it ceases to be metalled, with Dalegarth Hall away to your right – notice its sturdy round chimneys. Continue on to go through a gate and follow the track as it winds left. Ignore the bridleway that goes off left and right and stroll on to a gate on the left, signposted "Waterfall".

Pass through and follow the track that winds right. Walk the good track beside the tumbling stream on your left. In rhododendron time the bushes are a mass of bloom. Go slowly and quietly and you might come upon a mixed flock of long tailed tits, coal tits and goldcrests. Look up into the lofty trees for nuthatches, tree creepers and woodpeckers.

As you progress the gill becomes narrower and the sides immensely high. The sky is just a slit of blue and seemingly very far above. Soon all birdsong is blotted out by the noise of the hurrying beck. The view of the fall from above the third bridge is breathtaking. The beck hurtles over the lip of a crag and descends in an unbroken fall through riotous vegetation. Droplets of white spray sparkle in the sunshine and then they, and the turquoise water, are lost in the black plunge pool deep in a lush hollow. It is heaven indeed, but take care.

Return by your outward route.

Stanley Force

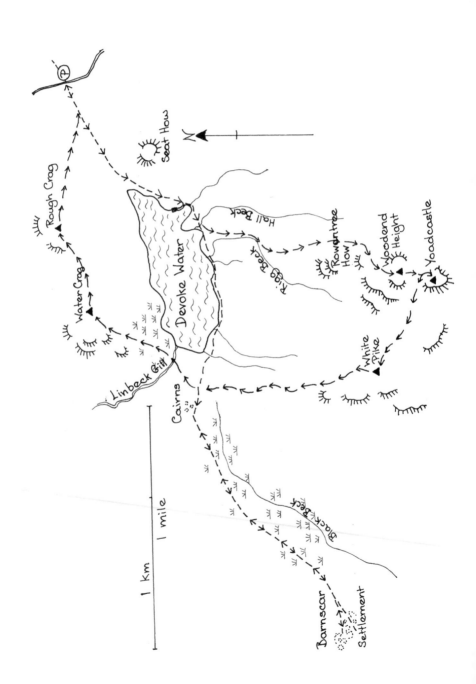

Rough Crag

Seat How

N

Water Crag

Hall Beck

Rigg Beck

Rowantree How

Woodend Height

Yoadcastle

Devoke Water

White Pike

Linbeck Gill

Cairns

Blackbeck

Barnscar

Settlement

1 Km

1 mile

Walk 5: Devoke Water – Barnscar

*Birker Fell – Boathouse – Woodend Heights – Yoadcastle – White Pike –
Devoke Water – Barnscar settlement – Devoke Water – Water Crag –
Rough Crag*

Start/finish: Verge parking (GR 172977) to the north-east of the Ulpha to Eskdale
Green road. The verge is close to the signpost at the highest point of the road as it traverses Birker Moor.

Type of walk: This is a challenging 8-miler, which starts with a pathless climb to a
grand top. The bridleway on the OS map to the atmospheric settlement of Barnscar is
quite good but after rain it can be miry in parts. The return is back along the bridleway,
over Ling Beck (which might present a problem if the tarn is very high after prolonged
rain) and then over two lesser heights.

Map: OS Outdoor Leisure 6 (new series).

Nearest towns: Millom, Broughton-in-Furness.

Public transport: None.

Refreshments and toilets: Millom, Broughton.

Cross the road from the parking area and continue ahead along a rough track Go
through a gate and stride on towards Devoke Water. The tarn is nearly a mile
long and half a mile wide, making it one of the largest in the Lake District. It belongs to the Penningtons of Muncaster Castle.

The track leads to a romantic two-storied boathouse and stable. It has a
small room where gillies looked after guests staying at the castle who liked to
visit the remote stretch of water.

Follow a narrower path, bearing off left, and walk on to cross two small
streams. Between the second, Hall Beck, and the third, Rigg Beck, look up to
see the cairn on Woodend Height (1597ft/487m). Strike up, for just over half-a
mile, the steadily rising, pathless fell, choosing the driest and easiest way, with
perhaps a pause on Rowantree How as you go.

Continue upwards to the cairned top and enjoy the magnificent view of the
tarn and of the many Lakeland summits. Go on in the same general direction,
across a col, and then climb the rocky cairnless top of Yoadcastle
(1610ft/491m), where you will wish to pause. Look for the Isle of Man sprawling
along the skyline.

Drop back down to the col and look towards the coast to see, half a mile
away, the columnar cairn on rocky White Pike (1370ft/418m). A generally clear
narrow path takes you across the high rough pasture to this delectable top.
Pause again and look for Muncaster Castle nestling on the edge of woodland –
ignore Sellafield nuclear power station if you can. Then descend the slopes, for
nearly 3/4 of a mile, to rejoin the path just beyond the foot of the tarn. Look for
some ancient cairns and try to avoid the wetter areas. Here you might disturb a
snipe probing for prey in the ooze.

Follow the bridleway, west, as it stretches away towards the sea. Where it disappears in mire use convenient stones or hop from tuft to tuft. Follow it for one mile, passing small clumps of stones and then a row of what might have been boundary stones or ancient marker posts, perhaps the outskirts of the early settlement named Barnscar on the map. At a Y-junction take the right branch to go through a vast area of the remains of round huts, boundary walls and burial mounds. What a large village it must have been. It was probably occupied several times from Bronze Age Man onwards. Successive occupants would have chosen this remote site to hide from invading Vikings, Scots and, possibly, Romans.

Return the mile or so along the bridleway to where you joined it. Then take a fairly clear track going off left and leading you to the side of Ling Beck, just above a charming waterfall. If the stream is low enough, step across it. If it is full, use your walking poles to help you balance across several convenient boulders.

Beyond, an indistinct path takes you across more mire to the foot of Water Crag (997ft/304m). It then continues upwards to its small cairn, from where the view is breathtaking. Go on across the heather-covered way, keeping parallel with the tarn on your right, to Rough Crag (1049ft/320m), its cairn atop granite boulders. From here there is a superb view of the lovely pool and the Lakeland mountains.

Then begin your gentle descent over the sheep pasture, keeping to the right of the rocky outcrop of Pike How, to join the track. Go on along it to regain the parking area.

Snipe

Walk 6: Whit Fell

Corney Fell Road – Buck Barrow – Guide Crag – Burn Moor – Whit Fell

Start/finish: At the highest point on the pass over Corney Fell is a large firm area for parking (GR149903). To reach this, leave the A595 by the fell road, west of Duddon Bridge.

Type of walk: This is a grand linear walk of 5½-miles in total. It is over high rough fell, with narrow indistinct paths, which can be wet in parts. It is a walk for a fine day to enjoy the extensive views into Scotland, Yorkshire, Wales, the Isle of Man and the Lake District. Because the walk starts from such a high point, it is difficult to realise as you stroll to the top of Whit Fell (1881ft/572m) that it is little more than 30 metres lower than Black Combe (see walk 7).

Map: OS Outdoor Leisure 6 (new series).

Nearest town/village: Millom, Broughton-in-Furness.

Public transport: None.

Refreshments/public toilets: Millom, Broughton.

Cross the road and walk north, with the fine wall to your left. A tractor-marked track makes for easy walking and from it are the first of many dramatic views of the Lake District giants – Dow Crag, Coniston Old Man, Crinkle Crags, Bowfell, Esk Pike, Great End and the Scafells.

As the track swings left, walk ahead to the foot of Buck Barrow (1799 ft/549m), a jagged hillock, spiking upwards, teeth-like, out of the rolling featureless moorland. This delightful hill can be seen from much of the Duddon Valley and it is good to stand on it for a change and look down on the lower land.

Scramble easily up this delightful crag, weaving between the rocks on rough pasture. Pause to look right to see the Howgills and Ingleborough and down into Lancashire and the Duddon estuary. Then go on up to a narrow boulder field that stretches between rock pinnacles on either side. Beyond, follow an indistinct path through more boulder strewn grass to cross Guide Crag.

Coniston Fells from Buck Barrow

Pause again to look left down to Ravenglass and, alas, Sellafield. From here you can see also the path that takes you across the flat damp moorland below and then climbs straight up to the cairn on Burn Moor (1780ft/543m). (NB. The wetter areas are clad in red-leafed cotton grass; the drier areas are composed of green matt grass, which tends to yellow as it ages.)

From Burn Moor St Bees Head comes into view and Scotland and you can look out across the Irish Sea to the Isle of Man. From the cairn look right (north east) for another clearish path crossing the ridge and climbing gently to the summit of Whit Fell (1881ft/572m). As you go you can see row after row of low ridges, stretching away to the east. The path leads you to the top, a glorious, flat airy summit, with a small rock shelter by the cairn and a trig point. From here the Ravenglass estuary looks like a relief map in an old geography book.

From the summit look slightly west of north, across the moorland below, to Holehouse Tarn. Beyond the fence, stands Stainton Pike. Due north lies Yoadcastle and White Pike (see Walk 5).

Return by the same route, but this time contour the slopes of Burn Moor to join the path across the moorland. Go right round Guide Crag and Buck Barrow, where a narrow path makes an easily spotted half circle. Join the cart track over the fell to the parking area.

Walk 7: Black Combe

*Whicham – Townend Knotts – Black Combe – Butcher's Breast – Fell
Cottage – Whitbeck Mill – Moor Gill –Whicham*

Start/finish: At the tiny settlement of Whicham, which lies on the A595 between
Broughton-in-Furness and Bootle. Park in a lay-by on the side of the A-road close to
Whicham church (GR 1136827).

Type of walk: This is an energetic 8-mile walk. At the foot of the fell the path climbs,
steeply at first, and then more easily. As you near the 1970ft /600m summit a short
path on the right leads to the trig point set in a shelter of rocks. A clearish path and
then a good track lead you down and down to the fell wall, where you turn left to return
below the sprawling giant of a mountain along paths and tracks.

Map: OS Outdoor Leisure 6 (new series).

Nearest towns: Millom, Broughton-in-Furness.

Public transport: Use the community bus, Muncaster Microbus 14, from Millom to
Muncaster, alighting at the garage at Whicham corner, and then walk up the lane to
the church. North Western Trains, from Barrow or Whitehaven, will bring you to
Silecroft station and then road and path walking will add just over half-a-mile to each
end of your walk (see map). Inquiries Cumbria Journey Planner 01228 60600.

Refreshments/toilets: Silecroft, Millom, Broughton.

From the lay-by walk past the church of St Mary's on your left. As you go notice
that it has a bell-cote with two bells, surmounted by a stone cross. To the right
of the church is a private house, which once was Whicham and Millom Gram-
mar School, founded in 1540. The space in front of the old school was once the
playground and there is room for careful parking here.

Walk between the church and the old school and, at the bottom of the steps,
turn left to stroll along a pleasing lane. Where the tarmac ceases continue along
a wide track passing behind a farm. Beyond, strike right, up the fell, to a stile and
a gate.

Once over the stile climb the wide grassy path that swings up the slopes. In
parts it is steep, giving you a good excuse to pause and look back over the
coastal plain below, its many pools and dykes sparkling in the luminous light.

Continue climbing, accompanied by the chattering of Moorgill Beck to the
right of the track. Ignore a narrow grassy path coming in on your left – this is
your return route. Here and there outcrops of Skiddaw slate, pink tinged, break
through the moorland turf. Once Townend Knotts is passed the upper fells
come into view and the path is seen in the distance, swinging away, left,
through heather and bilberry. Then the way climbs less steeply. Enjoy the extensive views across to the Pennines to the east and to the Isle of Man to the
west.

After a two mile climb from the church the track comes close to the summit.
Follow a narrow path that goes off right and scramble up to the trig point and
the shelter. On a good day Scotland, Wales, much of north-west England and

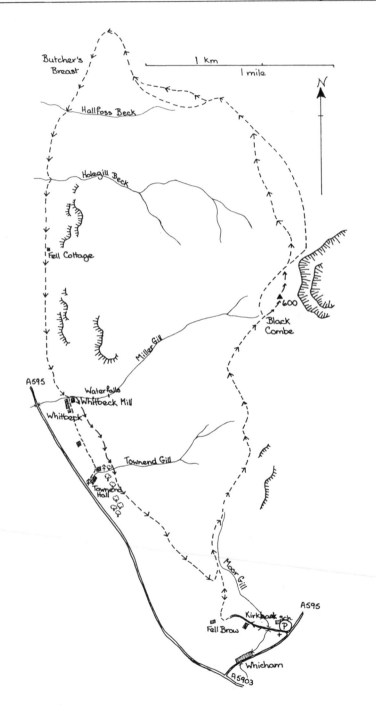

Butcher's
Breast

1 km

1 mile

N

Hallfoss Beck

Holegill Beck

Fell Cottage

Miller Gill

▲ 600

Black
Combe

A595

Waterfalls

Whitbeck Mill

Whitbeck

Townend Gill

Townend
Hall

Moor Gill

A595

Kirkbank sch.

P

Fell Brow

Whicham

A5903

even Ireland are visible. In the mist it is possible to be mesmerised by the good track and miss the summit altogether!

From the trig point walk due north, descending a gentler slope to join the track, walked earlier, but now you are further along it. As you descend you can see the continuing path that takes you across moorland to join a distinct track, which heads in the direction of the village of Bootle. This track divides several times but all ways come down the long gentle slope to unite at the side of a fence.

Turn left and continue beside a wall on your right. The distinct track leads below the wild craggy west face of the mountain, revealing much of its Skiddaw slate bedrock. Step across Hallfoss Beck and Holegill Beck and continue on. Pass below Tarn Dimples and then beside a small boarded up cottage.

Stride the track, keeping ahead when the wall and a path turn down right. The way soon comes beside a wall on the right and then to Whitbeck Mill, still with its huge waterwheel in position.

Walk on along the track for a few metres and take the steps on the left. Walk up the fell, with a pleasing view ahead of the waterfalls tumbling down Miller Gill. Take the first right turn, a grassy swathe through bracken. Ignore the right turn down to the track and go on. Where the way divides, continue on the path that runs parallel with the wall.

Whitbeck waterfalls

Descend to the beck that hurries down Townend Gill, step across and carry on to join a renovated track that climbs the fell. Follow this across the slopes of Townend Knotts and, at its end; go on along the continuing path. Follow it where it veers left and descends to the track taken earlier on the way to the summit.

Turn right and descend the steepish way to the gate and stile. Bear left along the track and then the road to return to the steps up to Whicham Church.

Walk 8: Annaside

Cumbria Coastal Way – Whitbeck – Gutterby – Annaside – Midtown farm-
Barfield – Fell Cottage – Whitbeck

Start/finish: The lay-by in front of Whitbeck Church on the A595, north-west of Millom (GR 119839.)

Type of walk: This 6½-miler along the Cumbrian coast, so different from the dramatic inland scene of Lakeland, has a quiet charm of its own. You will meet few people but see plenty of birds, sheep and cattle. Annaside Banks is one of Cumbria's pleasant secrets. The footpath traverses low cliffs and vast boulder-strewn beaches, part of the Cumbria Coastal Way. These sea-rounded boulders (cobbles) were once used for constructing the scattered farmhouses, their barns and turf dykes (walls). You return along a good track below the dramatic flanks of Black Combe. Generally easy to walk and well waymarked. Take care on the cliff path, which is frequently eroded. Repairs are never ending. Tracks can be muddy after rain.

Map: OS Outdoor Leisure 6 (new series).

Nearest town: Millom.

Public transport: No buses along the A595. North Western Trains, nearest station Silecroft, 2 miles from the start of the walk at Whitbeck, inquiries 0345 484950

Refreshments/toilets: Two inns at Silecroft and at Bootle – none en route.

From the parking area in front of the church, cross the A-road and take the sign-posted narrow lane towards Gutterby, which once was a spa. With care, cross the railway line and follow the continuing track, which swings right. Look right for a good view of Black Combe's western flank.

Continue past a copse of willow, sycamore, hawthorn and blackthorn. Stride on to pass Gutterby farm. Away to the right you can see the Muncaster Fell (Walk 2) and then the Irish Sea comes into view. Stroll on and, where the track swings sharp right, pass through a gate ahead.

Carry on to pass through another gate and along the gradually descending track. It continues to the shore but you leave by the stile on the right beside the next gate to walk right along the shallow cliffs.

Carry on the stiled way and then follow it, with care, across Bog Hole, a basin-shaped depression in the cliff. Look for redshanks, curlews and oyster catchers on the shore. Skylarks flit about the path before ascending into the air. Beyond the next stile, join a reinforced track and saunter along the low cliffs for just over a mile. Follow the track as it swings right towards the small settlement of Annaside. Head on to pass between the buildings of Midtown farm. Take the continuing hedged track that rises steadily, slightly to the right, beyond the farm gate.

Continue on the track almost to its end. Turn left towards a footbridge over the River Annas, but do NOT cross. Go right to walk a delightful permissive path. Pass under the sturdy three-arched bridge; the stone of its arches is placed aslant for strength. Beyond a gate, walk on beside the river to a corner

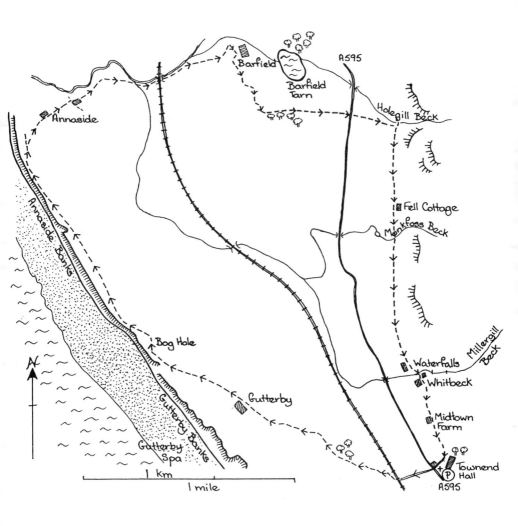

stile. Once over, follow the boundary fence to pass a gate and continue to a stile.

Beyond head diagonally right towards the dramatic ruin of Barfield House, once a fine mansion. It was built by Joseph Huddleston, a member of the prominent family that lived at Millom Castle. The family supported the king in the civil war and because of this lost all their money; some lost their lives. Behind the old house lies the reed-fringed Barfield Tarn, shadowed by willows and alders.

Continue along the track as it swings right in front of the ruin and go on to pass through a gate to a reinforced lane. Turn left to walk to the A595. Cross

with care and take the
signposted gate oppo-
site. Continue beside a
wall on your left and go on
to pass through two
gates.

Turn right onto a track,
keeping parallel with the
wall on your right, below
the forbidding slopes of
bracken-clad   Black
Combe. Look right across
the hinterland, and the
sea, to see Snaefell on the
Isle of Man. Pass a tiny
cottage tucked under the
steep slopes, and stride
on below the cascading
falls in Monkfoss Gill.

Stroll on along the high
level track and then follow
it as it drops down the
slope and continues be-
side a fine curving wall to
reach Whitbeck Mill. Be-
yond the mill stride the
wide cart track and follow

Whitbeck Mill

it as it slowly descends to pass another farm named Midtown, and then
Townend Hall farm, back to Whitbeck Church to rejoin your car.

Walk 9: White Combe

Beckside – Whitecombe Beck – Whitecombe Head – White Combe –
Cross Bank – Beckside

Start/finish: There is room for several cars in a council lay-by at Beckside on the A595 (GR 153847).

Type of walk: An excellent 4½-miler that takes you up a delightful path into the lonely environs of Whitecombe Beck. It continues over high flattish moorland to the cairn, where spectacular views await. The return is down ancient grooved ways and then paths and tracks to the parking area, avoiding all but a brief dalliance with the busy A-road.

Map: OS Outdoor Leisure 6 (new series).

Nearest town: Millom.

Public transport: Not convenient. If you use the F73 community bus, Millom to Muncaster you will have to walk the A595 from Whicham to Beckside. Using North Western Trains to Silecroft will involve you in a much longer trek to start the walk. Inquiries Cumbria Journey Planner 01228 60600

Refreshments/toilets: Millom, Silecroft, Broughton.

From the lay-by cross the road to take a pleasing track past Ralliss farm. Go through a gate and continue on past Whicham Mill, now a private house set among trees. Follow the track beside a magnificent wooded area where, through the trees, you can see the beck tumbling down to the mill in tempestuous falls. Continue along a bank to pass through the fell gate into the lonely valley.

Cross Whitecombe Beck on a tractor bridge and walk on the rising track, once an old mine road. Continue on the now high-level way with the beck below and the fell slopes rising steeply on either side. Step across the cascades of Blackcombe Beck and peer upstream to see the formidable Blackcombe

The summit of White Combe

Screes. Stroll on along the good track and then pause by a huge boulder to look down on a pretty pool and fall below.

Take the lower path, where the way divides, to come to the side of the beck. Step across at a convenient place to take the zigzagging path ascending ahead. Follow it as it winds up the side of the steep slope, with a fine view across the valley of Whitecombe Screes. As the path comes to the highest part of the fell, take an indistinct path turning acute right (due south), to walk the rough grassy ridge of White Combe.

From the footpath across the fell there is a wonderful view ahead across Morecambe Bay. Then follow the tractor path that leads you in the same general direction. The cairn on top of the fell disappears for a short time, but soon

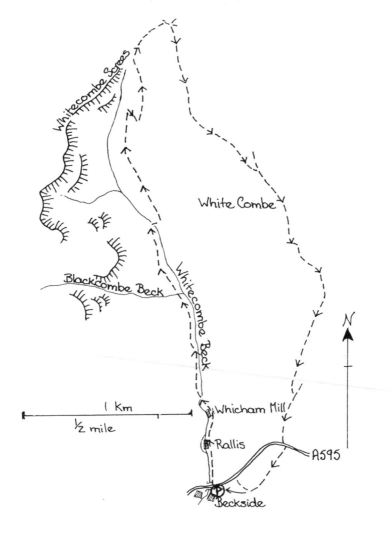

comes into view again over the flat fell and a path leads you to it. From this grand summit you have an intimate view into the Duddon estuary and an extensive one across the bay and the Lakeland Fells.

Pause awhile in the lee of the shelter-cum-cairn and then bear left (east) down the slope to join an old drove road that runs in a groove and winds steadily downhill below White Hill Knott. Some of the grooves are deep and filled with bracken and the paths run along the banking. At places there are several grooves to choose from but all go on downhill, quite gently, first over grassy fell and then through extensive swathes of bracken.

Go on downhill on the raised path and follow it as it swings left to a gate in the far corner, giving access to a track between hedgerows. Turn right and enjoy the pleasant way. The last ten yards are always abominably muddy and you will have to step carefully to reach the gate to the A595.

Cross the road with extreme care and walk left for a few metres to an easy-to-miss stile just back from a purposely-left gap between the end of the hedge and the start of a wall. Once over, head across the pasture to join a track, where you walk right. Go through the next gate and walk on past a small quarry. Take a grassy track climbing right to go through a gate on the left. Edge right, round the pasture, to come to a gate into the farmyard at Beckside. Then take another gate on the right to the lay-by from where the walk started.

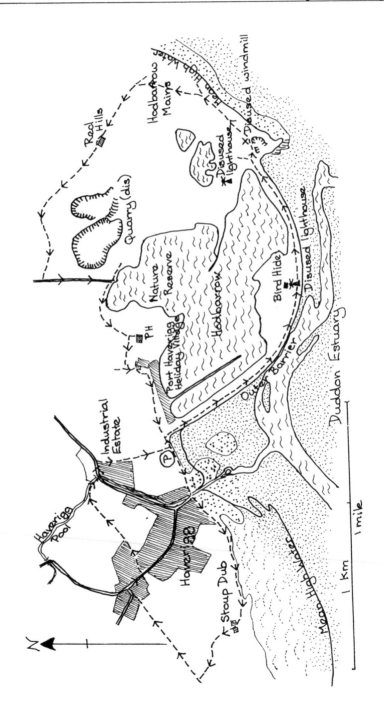

Walk 10: Haverigg

Haverigg – Stoup Dub farm – Haws Lane – Industrial Estate – Outer Barrier – Hodbarrow Mains – Redhills – Steel Green – Haverigg

Start/finish: Rough ground overlooking the seashore, to the west of Port Haverigg Holiday Village (GR 164786). By car, approach the seashore as far as the roundabout in Haverigg village and then cross the bridge over the River Lazey, just before it enters the sea.

Type of walk: This 7-mile walk is dominated for almost all the way by the sprawling mass of Black Combe. The village of Haverigg, from where the walk starts, dates from the 12th century. It is a picturesque corner of coastal Cumbria and is full of interest. The walk is well waymarked. Much of it is on good tracks. Part of it crosses the almost pathless Hodbarrow Mains. There is an exciting stretch along the Outer Barrier from where there are good views of relicts of Hodbarrow Mine. You also pass a sturdy bird hide on the way, which is well worth a visit.

Map: OS Outdoor Leisure 6 (new series).

Nearest town: Millom.

Public transport: Stagecoach Cumberland from Millom to Haverigg, inquiries 01846 63222. Good connecting buses from Millom North Western Trains station to Haverigg, rail inquiries 0345 484950.

Refreshments: Haverigg and Millom

Toilets: Beside recreation ground at Haverigg.

From the parking area on the rough ground, walk west, on the Cumbria Coastal Way (CCW), towards the tall white holiday homes overlooking the tiny harbour. Continue on the shore side of these to cross the bridge over the River Lazey. Bear round left and then right to follow the shore road. Pass between the cafe and the recreation ground and toilets and on past the Inshore Rescue, now with extensive sand dunes to the left.

Stroll on ahead on the metalled track, with a fine view of Black Combe, White Combe and Millom Park. Then pass the Rugby Club and higher dunes to the left. Go on ahead, when the track ceases to be metalled, and pass the farmhouse of Stoup Dub. Turn right, immediately beyond it, to walk between the dwelling and its outbuildings and stride on, bearing slightly left on a grassy track. Follow it as it swings left to a good stile, beside a gate. Beyond, continue in the same general direction to the far corner and a stile, which gives access to Haws Lane.

Turn right and saunter ahead along the track to join North Lane Turn right and, after a few metres, join Haverigg main street. Cross the road and walk right to take a left turn, Sandham Lane. At its end carry on ahead on the continuing unmade track. Where the lane turns sharp left, press on along a gated reinforced path that keeps to the side of a pasture, with a hedge to your right. Enjoy the view of Black Combe. As you reach the brow of the path you have a pleasing view of Millom, with its houses gathered around its fine church.

The path brings you beside Haverigg Pool and then in a few metres you join the main road to Haverigg, which you cross. Turn left and then right to walk beside the Industrial Estate on your right. Go ahead until you reach the shore. Turn left to walk the CCW and continue where it goes on towards the sea. Bear round left to walk between the lagoon and the sea and pause.

In the 1850s mining for iron-ore began at Hodbarrow Point. To protect the mine from being flooded by the sea a wooden barrier was erected in 1885 and, three years later, work began on an inner sea wall. In 1889 the sea breached this wall, the remnants of which can be seen as you look inland, and an outer barrier was constructed from Haverigg to Hodbarrow Point. This is what you are walking on.

It was built of limestone rubble and 25-ton concrete blocks. They were made nearby and all were numbered – with care you can still see the numbers. Work continued at the mine until it closed in 1968.

Half-way along the outer barrier you pass the bird hide on your left and, on the shoreside, the old lighthouse. At the end on the inner barrier you can see an earlier lighthouse. Ahead stands a ruined windmill. Both the windmill and the stone lighthouse, reminiscent of Victorian follies, stand on grassy eminences.

Walk on around the outer barrier and continue where, for a few metres, the track turns inland. Look for the CCW signpost, on the right, leave the main track and climb over the grassy slope, keeping to the left of the windmill. This leads to a hedged track that descends towards the shore. Go through the gate and turn right to pass through a kissing gate with a solid iron gate. Continue along the boulder-strewn shore and step onto the turf banking, just beyond a wall on the left. Head inland to come to a fence. Turn right and follow it until you reach a track heading left.

Wind round, with the fence to your left, and follow the track to another that goes on beyond a signposted stile and gate. Walk the good track to pass a dwelling named Red Hills. Carry on towards Millom church tower and Black Combe, which lie directly ahead. Ignore any footpaths off and keep on the track as it swings left. Notice the great spoil heaps on your left from the old mine and go on to the road.

Turn left and then, at the end of the road, turn right. Walk on along the quiet reinforced lane to pass The Commodore, an inn, on your left. Bear left just beyond it and go on along the lane. Follow it where it swings right and ceases to be metalled. Descend the delightful way to wind round a dwelling with a colourful garden to reach the edge of Haverigg holiday village. Turn right and walk on to return to the rough ground from where you started your walk.

Common terns at Hodbarrow

Walk 11: Millom Park

*The Green – The Hill – School Ellis – Millom Park – Dunningwell –
The Green*

Start/finish: Grass verge or roadside opposite the Punch Bowl Inn at The Green, Millom Without (GR 179846).

Type of walk: This 7-miler takes in two contrasting environs. Part of the walk is over delightful pastures and gentle fell and the other is through the mixed woodland of Millom Park. This is the only remnant of the former hunting park of Millom Castle. Both sections provide easy walking, but expect plenty of mud after rain as you walk the pastures and pass through farms. Tracks are generally good through the forest.

Map: OS Outdoor Leisure 6 (new series).

Nearest town: Millom.

Public transport: North Western Trains, Barrow/Carlisle. Alight at Green Road Station – by request. Walk left along the lane to reach the Punch Bowl. Inquiries 0345 484950. Stagecoach Cumberland bus services 7 and 507, inquiries 01946 63222.

Refreshments: Punch Bowl Inn, The Green; cafes and pubs at Millom and at Broughton-in-Furness.

Public toilets: Millom and Broughton.

Cross the road from the Punch Bowl to climb the narrow, hedged road opposite. This takes you among delightful undulating pastures, about which are scattered many outcrops of lichened rock. After 365 metres turn left onto a walled track, signposted "Cherry Tree". Go through a gate into a sheep pasture to take a stile on the right, just before a wooded hill. Bear left to climb the next ladder stile at the edge of the trees. Walk ahead over hillocky ground, bearing steadily right to walk beside a wall on your right. Go through a gate in this wall.

Head on right to pass through another unmarked gate to rough ground be-

Black Combe from Millom Park

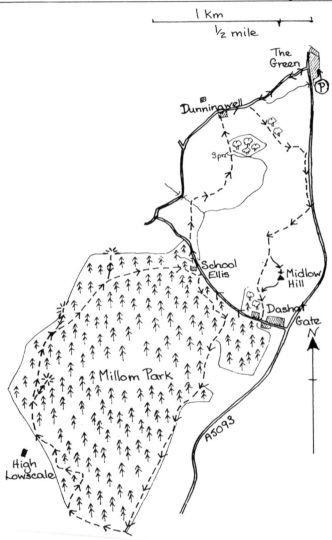

side the A-road. Walk right along a reinforced track (the old road) parallel with the main road to take a narrow lane leading off right, towards Woodhouse and Greenhills. The signpost stands on the opposite side of the A-road. Beyond the last bungalow (the second left turn of the OS map), bear left and walk beside a wall on the left. Ignore a gate on your left. Continue on to a ladder stile at the end of a short walled way. The right of way continues by the wall on the right. If you wish to climb Midlow Hill, climb steadily left towards a telegraph pole and then right to reach its tiny 90 metre summit – a glorious view of the Duddon estuary awaits. Drop down the steepish slope, right, to go through a gap in the wall.

Walk left towards a house and then pass it on your right. Climb the signposted stile to join a narrow road. Turn right to walk the delightful leafy lane. Just before a row of cottages, turn left to pass through the car park for the forest walk. Beyond the waymarked gate, walk ahead to start your circular walk in a clockwise direction. Follow the waymarks directing you left. As you approach a wall with a pasture beyond, swing right to take an easy-to-miss stone stile in the wall that brings you to the edge of the quarry.

Walk the path under larch trees, with dramatic glimpses of the quarry below. Cross the quarry access road and go on along a path into deciduous woodland. Watch for a large mound of quarry waste on which you can stand for a good view of the estuary. The waymarks lead you on through trees to the edge of the forest and a kissing gate to pastures. Turn right to take a wooden stile and climb the steepish slope to a stone-stepped stile. Negotiate the next stile and then turn right to walk a metalled way – a farm access track. Go on to climb a stone-stepped stile in the wall on your right to re-enter the forest.

Walk ahead for 23 metres and then bear left to continue your circular stroll. Pass a pretty tarn away to the right and at this point the waymarks direct you left. Climb the steepish slope and continue to a tall post. Leave the main path and climb right to a clearing in the trees. Here stands a huge balustraded wooden platform. Climb the two step ladders for a breathtaking view, which includes the Isle of Man.

Return to the main path and walk on. Three hundred metres off to the left is another viewpoint, with a glimpse into the Whicham Valley. Carry on along the main path and leave it left again for yet another viewpoint, and then return to the main path. Saunter on to the gate, leaving by the way you entered the forest. Turn left along the narrow lane and take the signposted stile on the right. Press on ahead to climb a ladder stile. Walk ahead to another stile into a walled pasture. Head towards a barn, which you pass on your right. Join a reinforced track and turn right.

Carry on to pass in front of Applehead farmhouse. Ignore the stile to the right, pass a barn and go through a waymarked gate to a walled way. Cross a damp area on a planked footbridge to climb a waymarked step stile. Beyond, bear left and continue through a short walled track to a gate. Turn left to take the next gate on your left and then climb a stile on your right. Keep to the left of the farmhouse and join the road, where you turn right to walk the lane back to the start.

Walk 12: Arnaby

A595 – Gornal Ground – Lady Hall – Duddon estuary embankment –
Strands – Arnaby – Hallthwaites – A595.

Start/finish: Park in the "old road" parallel to and north west of the A595 (GR 185867). The walk starts from this quiet lane, which lies east of Black Beck. The A595 winds its way from Grizebeck, by-passes Broughton-in-Furness and continues to Millom.

Type of walk: This is a most enjoyable 5-mile walk, with lots of contrasting views along unfrequented tracks and paths. Its stiles have been excellently refurbished and its little footbridges, over deepish ditches, have been covered with anti-slip wire mesh. Well waymarked.

Map: OS Outdoor Leisure 6 (new series).

Nearest towns: Millom. Broughton-in-Furness.

Public transport: Stagecoach Cumberland bus number 507 or 7, schooldays only, from Millom or Broughton, pass the start of the walk, inquiries 01946 63222. Or take North Western Trains from Millom or Barrow and start walk at Green Road station, just south east of the hamlet of Strands, inquiries 0345 484950.

Refreshments/toilets: Millom, Broughton, The White Horse Inn at The Hill.

From the "old road" take the gap stile to the left of the gate and stride across the narrow pasture to a stile through a hedgerow bordering the A595. Cross the busy road with extreme caution and walk ahead down the track, signposted Gornal Ground. Follow it as it winds right to pass a fine house. Enjoy the magnificent view of the estuary and the lush pastures and woodland that clothe the hinterland.

Pass through the nearer gate to take the lower of two waymarked tracks; here you might see nuthatches and long tailed tits. Go with the wall as it curves left and drops downhill to the side of a small hurrying beck. Cross on a little plank bridge and turn left to climb through the gap stile in the wall to join a track. Turn right to walk through the pleasing deciduous woodland, where bluebells grow in great profusion in the spring.

As you go look for the gap in the wall on the left through which a small stream makes its way to join the main beck. Here a variety of ferns thrive in the moist environment. To the right the beck drops in a series of pretty falls.

At the road, turn left and walk into the hamlet of Lady Hall. Continue past the phone box and turn right opposite a dwelling named Newton farm. Descend the rough slope beside a wall on your right to a short grassy track that goes off in the right corner. Look for the stone gap stile beside some corrugated iron and pass through. Stride ahead to the gate in the next hedge to pass through another squeeze stile.

Beyond walk steadily right to a gated footbridge over High Shaw Pool, which receives water from the small beck crossed earlier on the walk. Look left from the bridge to see the ladder stile, which gives access to the way across the

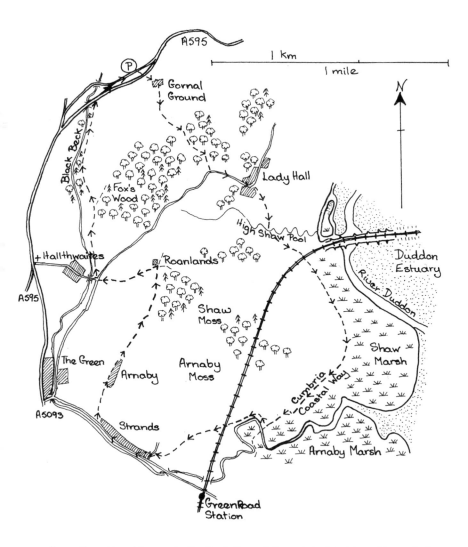

railway line. Head towards it, climb the white painted ladder stile and observe the request to take great care and to look both ways before you cross.

Climb the ladder stile on the far side of the line and walk ahead a few metres to a waymark. This directs you left onto an embankment, where you walk right along the Cumbria Coastal Way. This glorious raised grassy way gives you a splendid view of the Duddon estuary. Look back before the embankment curves right to see the railway viaduct strung out dramatically across the river.

Continue on the high level easy-to-walk way. Small reedy pools reflect the scudding clouds. Shelduck, wild geese and oyster catchers feed in the tidal gutters. Meadow pipits flit about the marsh and rise often, carolling into the sky. Look for the waymark directing you right, off the embankment onto a farm track where you continue to a wide plank bridge over a large meander of Black Beck, just before it joins the estuary. Do not cross but take the waymarked stile on the right.

The path continues on the embankment of the beck and here in a tidal pool you might see a kingfisher feeding before it flies off with a flash of metallic blue, its short rounded wings whirring rapidly. The embankment curves right and then left and brings you to another pair of ladder stiles that enable you to cross the railway line once again.

Kingfisher

Walk ahead on an indistinct path through bracken, with Arnaby Moss stretching away right, to cross a plank footbridge. Here, in spring, the bushes resound with the songs of migrants. Go on to a second plank bridge over the wider ditch, on your left, and climb the stile into a pasture. Go diagonally right across the field to another stile. Continue beside the hedge on your right to a third stile. Beyond, bear right across a field to a gate into a track. Turn left to walk to a road.

Turn right to carry on through the hamlet of Strands. Look left, as you go, to see several short flights of steps that lead to the top of the banking of the beck and then down the other side into the stream itself – perhaps for villagers to obtain water, or do their washing, in years gone by.

Head on past an attractive dry stone bridge to a small green, where you turn right to take a narrow hedged lane, signposted Arnaby. Go past Tarn Bank and then, at Arnaby Cottage, take the right fork. Where it divides again keep to the left branch and stroll along the hedged and walled track. It passes through quiet pastures and from it there are delightful views over this attractive corner of Cumbria.

Ignore the track to the right and continue on the narrow grassy gated path between walls. Then leave the track through a wide gap on the right, to head for the obvious waymark in a wall across a pasture and near to the corner of the birch woodland of Shaw Moss. Continue ahead through another gateless gap and then a wall stile to come to Roanlands farm, where a tall post supports three waymarks.

Turn left and go through a gate. Climb straight up the slope, by the wall to your left, to a gap stile in the wall corner at the start of more deciduous woodland. Continue on, keeping parallel with the walled wood, to a magnificent step stile into the wood at the far edge of the trees. This gives access to a splendid track that takes you gently downhill to the hamlet of Hallthwaites which, together with The Green and Ladyhall, forms the parish of Thwaites.

Here at Hallthwaites was a thriving woollen mill that is believed to have dated back to the 16th century. Carpets and blankets were woven and dyed, the mill using the energy derived from the fast flowing Black Beck, which rises on the fells and empties into the Duddon.

Cross the road and take the signposted track on your right, signposted Thwaites Mill. To your left hurries Black Beck, where you will often see a dipper. Go through the stile beside the gate and continue beside the wall on your right. Pass through the gate at the end of the wall to walk a track beside the trees of Fox's Wood. Notice the old reinforced stone edging of the woodland boundary.

Leave the woodland by a stone stile and walk ahead, keeping beside the ruined wall on your left. Away to your left you can hear, but not see, the lively Black Beck. The indistinct path comes beside a small coniferous plantation with steep slopes dropping down to the beck.

Pass through two gates and cross the A595, again with great care. Walk a few steps ahead towards Thwaites Mill, once a flour mill, now a dwelling. Turn right to rejoin your car.

Walk 13: Duddon Iron Furnace and Swinside Circle

Old road at Broadgate – A595 – Graystone House – Boadhole – Furnace Woods – Duddon Furnace – Furnace Woods – Corney Fell – Swinside Circle – Broadgate

Start/finish: The disused section of the old Millom road, close to the A595 turn-off for Broadgate (GR 180865)

Type of walk: An exciting 7-miler to visit two historic reminders of South Cumbria's past. After a short unavoidable stretch along the A595 the route takes you over the fell, through delightful deciduous woodland and along very quiet narrow roads.

Map: OS Outdoor Leisure 6 (new series).

Nearest town: Millom, Broughton-in-Furness.

Public transport: Limited service, Stagecoach Cumberland, inquiries 01946 63222 (See walk 12).

Refreshments/toilets: Broughton and Millom.

Duddon blast furnace was built in 1736 and required a large number of workers to toil all year round to produce charcoal or wrest iron from the ore that arrived by barge at the mouth of the Duddon river. Each working day two tons of cast iron was produced.

Fifty-one stones of the Swinside Circle remain erect; many heavily encrusted with lichen. Why did our ancestors, Neolithic man, 3,500 years ago, choose such a bleak windswept area, 240 metres above sea level? Perhaps the climate was warmer and Black Combe provided all the shelter that was needed.

Swinside Stone Circle

The Walk

Walk north-east (in the direction of Broughton) along the old road until it joins the A595. Continue on along the grass verge, with care, for 200 metres to take the first left turn, a track that leads to Graystone House. Keep above the farmhouse. Climb steadily, ignoring any tracks off left. Pass through two gates and stride on towards Boadhole, a small farmhouse on your left. Use the ladder stile to climb the boundary wall of the grassy area in front of the dwelling and then al-

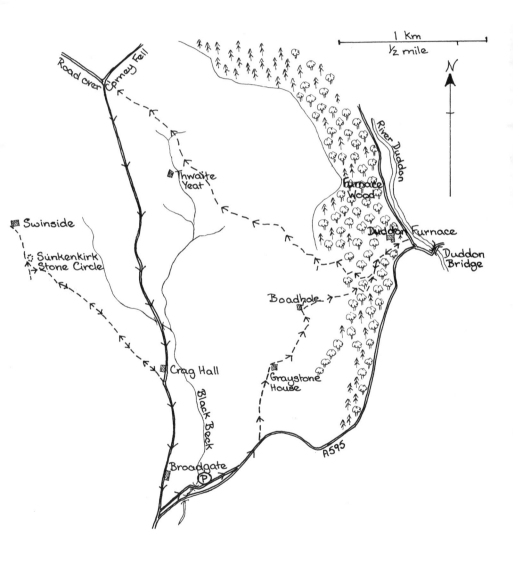

most immediately re-cross the wall by a second ladder stile, a manoeuvre made necessary by the rather eccentric right-of-way.

Follow the footpath as it strikes half left, avoiding any intervening damp ground. Just before you reach a lime kiln, which is on private ground, continue left and walk through gorse scrub. Go on to a ladder stile in the boundary wall of Duddon Woods. Once among the trees turn right and then, where the path branches and is waymarked, take the left fork.

The delightful path drops steadily downhill through the glorious woodland. It then curves left and remains on the same contour for a tenth of a mile, to a waymark at the side of a stream. Cross, turn right and descend the pleasing track, which is occasionally cobbled. This is an old packhorse route along which ore was carried to the furnace. Cross the driveway that leads to a holiday complex and go on through the trees (waymarked) to come to the furnace. Wander around the unexpectedly grand 18th century structure. It has been superbly excavated, consolidated and restored. An informative display panel will enhance your explorations.

Return back along the cobbled path but do not cross the stream where you did previously; instead go ahead as directed by another waymark. The indistinct way climbs steadily through ancient coppiced oak and hazel, keeping close to a wall on your right. A good track soon emerges and continues its zigzagging way, uphill.

Leave the woods by a gate and walk ahead through bracken. The clear way continues to zigzag to ease the gradient. Where the path forks, take the waymarked right branch. Go on to pass through a gate in the wall. Stroll on along a short walled way and then continue to a gate onto the open fell. Turn left and stay with the wall on your left to stride a wide grassy track, with dramatic views ahead of White Combe and Black Combe.

Pass through old slate spoil from a small quarry. Where the wall drops away left to Thwaite Yeat farm, go on ahead over the open fell. Aim for the narrow fell road across the pasture. The path gets lost in mire for a short section, but reappears again. Follow it to join the road at the point where it turns sharp right to go over the pass.

Pause here to enjoy the dramatic view of the Coniston range and then turn left to walk the narrower road, virtually traffic-free, signposted Broadgate. Stroll down the lovely way for just over a mile to pass Crag Hall farm. Just beyond, turn right to climb a farm track, which ascends steeply at first and then levels out. The track continues over Knott Moor and, after three-quarters of a mile from the fell road, crosses a cattle grid and goes through a gate. Beyond, through a gate on the right, stands the stone circle. Here Herdwicks use the stones as scratching posts.

After you have looked your fill, return down the access track. Turn right to continue down the narrow road. Just before it joins the A595, turn left to rejoin your car.

Walk 14: Frith Hall

Layby – Woodyard – River Duddon – Holehouse Gill Beck – Bobbin Mill –
Bleabeck Bridge – Frith Hall – Ulpha Park woods – Logan Beck Bridge –
Layby

Start/finish: Layby opposite entrance to Duddon Hall. This lies just under a mile along the Corney Fell road, from Duddon Bridge (GR 193896)

Type of walk: A pleasing 4½-mile walk on a level path through woods and over open fell. The return requires a steepish climb up a very quiet road and then another up to Frith Hall, but most of the return is level or downhill. Some road walking.

Map: OS Outdoor Leisure 6, The English Lakes – south west (new series)

Nearest town: Millom, Ulverston, Broughton-in-Furness.

Public transport: School buses, Millom to Broughton. Get off at Duddon Bridge and walk up fell road. Inquiries Stagecoach Cumberland 01946 63222

Refreshments and toilets: Broughton.

From the lay-by walk up the Corney Fell road to take, on the right, a signposted wide track. Follow it as it drops down to pass between a cottage and several buildings. Go on to cross a cobbled bridge over Logan Beck and then go on through the timber yard. Stride the track as it bears left and continues on the lower edge of the woodland of Ulpha Park, with pleasing pastures stretching away to your right. Then the waymarked path moves into woodland. Stroll on the wide way, which can be muddy after rain, to where the Duddon comes close beside the track. Cross the tractor bridge over Blea Beck and emerge from the trees onto open fell, with a wall to the right. Ahead The Pike, peaks proudly above Rainsborrow Wood.

Go with the track as it swings left, continuing beside Holehouse Gill Beck, a tributary of the Duddon. Pass through the gate and walk on to join the narrow fell road. Opposite, with its fine chimney intact, stands Ulpha bobbin mill, now a private house. It once provided the Lancashire cotton mills.

Turn left and begin the short fierce climb up the fell road. When the way levels look out for the signposted gate on the left. Go through and pause to enjoy the majestic view of the Seathwaite valley, stretching away to your left. Walk ahead along the grassy track, with the wall to your right. Then a fine view of the ruins of Frith Hall can be seen ahead.

Frith Hall

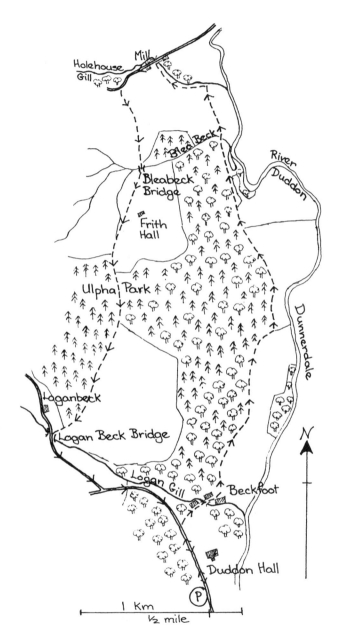

Cross a picturesque stone bridge over Blea Beck and continue on the wide track to come below the now dangerous ruins. Frith Hall was built in 1608 as a hunting lodge for the Huddleston family. Later it became an inn, a good stopping place for the packhorse trains to change their ponies, and for refreshment, on their way to Millom on the old coaching road over Corney Fell. It is also believed to have been the local Gretna Green, and in 1730 a dozen or so "marriages" were performed.

Remain on the gated track to enter Ulpha Park woods again. The lovely way goes on and on and then emerges below the slopes of Penn, a fine hill, with scattered outcrops, heather and bracken. The track descends steadily to a gate to the road. Turn left and cross Logan Beck Bridge. Walk on to a road junction. Turn left, cross the cattle grid and continue down the shady road to rejoin your car.

Walk 15: Ulpha – River Duddon

Ulpha – Birks Wood – Kiln Bank – Hall Bridge – Crook Wood – Grimcrag ruin – Brighouse farm – Grimecrag Bridge – Hazel Head farm – Ulpha.

Start/finish: Open ground on the east side of the narrow road from Broughton-in-Furness before it crosses Ulpha Bridge over the River Duddon. Please observe requests on where not to park (GR 197929).

Type of walk: This delightful 5½-miler takes you through a secluded part of the lovely Duddon valley. A fine track crosses the skirts of Stickle Pike and then a footpath carries on below Caw. At Hall Bridge, which strides the Duddon, you begin your return, first along the road, and then on narrow paths through ancient deciduous woodland, where trees partially hide and soften quarry spoil. The return route is mainly well waymarked.

Map: OS Outdoor Leisure 6 The English Lakes, south western area (new series).

Nearest town: Broughton-in-Furness.

Public transport: Post bus from Broughton village, inquiries 01229 716220.

Refreshments and toilets: Broughton.

The tiny scattered village of Ulpha is approached by a winding hilly road from Duddon Bridge or by an equally winding one from Cockley Beck. The name Ulpha is believed to come from the Scandinavian, meaning, "wolf hill".

The Walk

Having parked in the area described, walk a few meters in the direction of Broughton (west) and take, on the left, the signposted bridleway for Kiln Bank. Climb steadily up the fell slopes where numerous outcrops of rock support lemon-coloured lichen, with a tumbling beck to the left.

Go past Birks House and continue to a gate into Birks Wood to walk the delightful needle-strewn path through the trees. Here huge boulders are heavily clothed in moss.

Emerge from the trees by a gate and take the right fork going on with a wall to your left. To your right the fell slopes are clad with scattered deciduous trees. Pass several Scots pine in a walled enclosure. This was once a Quaker burial ground and the wall had flag-stones let into it at a height where people could sit. Go on past a pretty fall. Stroll the delightful gated way out onto the open fell. As you approach a farmhouse, ignore the signposted path on the left and walk on to the right of the dwelling to join a narrow road.

Cross and go on along the continuing track. Stride the bridge over Tommy Gill beck. Go through the gate and stroll on below the steepish lower skirts of Caw. After initial muddiness where cattle have trampled, the way continues through bracken and rocky outcrops cradling holly, with glimpses of the river below.

Pass through a gate in a fence and stroll on to descend a splendid buttressed path that winds down to the valley floor, with its many enclosed pastures. Cross the stream, Black Sike, by a clapper bridge by the wall on the left. Look upstream to see a small arched bridge and another clapper, both just right for lambs to cross the beck. Follow the wall round right to pass left of Low Hall. Stride its access track left to rejoin the narrow road crossed earlier.

Turn right and continue to the road junction. Here walk left in the direction of Broughton, crossing Hall Bridge over the river. Walk on for 600 metres, facing oncoming traffic, with a grand view of Stickle Pike ahead and Caw to your left. Just after a dwelling named Crowberry, take the easy-to-miss narrow stepped stile in the wall, on the right, and head up the pasture, very slightly left, to take a gate into the ancient Crook Wood.

Holly

Without the waymarks it would be difficult to find your way. Walk straight up from the gate on a rough wet track to the first waymark. Go on straight up for a few more steps to a second marker, where you turn left. The next waymark, at the foot of a quarry spoil heap, sends you right and then left, curving round the base of the tip. Follow the narrow path as it winds left to pass in front of two roofless quarry huts. Beyond, tucked up close to a wall, is a wooden stile over a fence.

Once over, pass through a gate to dawdle a pleasing path over the fell to the foot of two more spoil heaps. At a T-junction of paths, just before the heaps, turn right and go on along the path. To the right, almost hidden in the trees on the right, is the huge quarry from where all the spoil came. At the foot of another spoil heap, climb the waymarked stile and walk right to the next waymark. This directs you left along a terrace on the side of the huge heap.

Pass in front of a roofless hut, on your right, and head up right to a stile in the fence, slightly obscured from view by the vegetation and the slope. Go on ahead along an indistinct path, keeping close to the outcrops at the foot of The Haws. Go through a gateless gap and continue on the driest way you can find towards a copse of trees, to walk (with the wall to your left) behind the picturesque, but unsafe ruin of Grimcrag farm.

Bear left at the end of the old dwelling and then right to keep parallel with the wall on the right, to pass through a waymarked gate (ignore the gate not waymarked). Stride ahead to the side of Brighouse farm, it too making an attractive scene, with its red-roofed barn. Turn left to stride its access track and then, as the track swings right to a bridge, leave it and go ahead to climb two stepped stiles through field boundaries. Beside you, as you continue, Crosby Gill beck descends in some delightful falls.

Cross the glorious stone Grimecrag Bridge (as spelt on the OS map) and walk the good cart track, left, to come to Hazel Head farm. Pass through two gates, ignoring the access lane to the road. Bear left to pass the farmhouse on

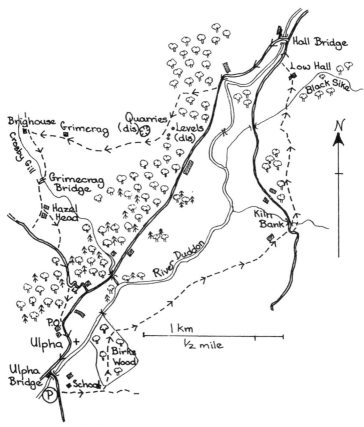

your right and go on with a barn to your left and walls to your right. After the last building move out into a pasture and continue with the wall on your right. Pass through a gate on your right and stroll on, towards the right corner of the deciduous woodland ahead, where a waymark, and then a signposted gate, give access to the fell road.

Turn left and descend gently to the first sharp corner, then take, on your right, a stile into more woodland. Descend the track, which is often wet, and treacherously covered with bronzed leaves, to a stile and then a ladder stile, just beyond, to descend to a pasture. Continue by the wall on your right and then, at the boundary wall, descend left to the road by the post office and store at Ulpha.

Walk right to come to the church, which stands on a small hillock overlooking the Duddon. The simple building is dedicated to St John and dates from the early 15th century. Inside, its white walls are a perfect foil for the blackened timbers of the roof. When it was redecorated in 1934, wall paintings were revealed, one showing the Arms of Queen Anne.

After leaving the church, walk on to cross Ulpha Bridge to rejoin your car.

Walk 16: Seathwaite

Seathwaite church – High Wallowbarrow – Rowantree How – Grassguards – Troutal – Tongue House – Long House – Turner Hall farm – Seathwaite

Start/finish: Park in a grassy lay-by nearly opposite Seathwaite Church, (GR 229962). The hamlet of Seathwaite is approached from the A590 by the fell road that runs north, leaving the A-road on the east side of Duddon Bridge; or from Cockley Beck if you have traversed the very narrow road over Hardknott Pass or Wrynose Pass.

Type of walk: This 5½-mile walk takes you through the secret corners of the lovely Duddon Valley. There is a steepish climb beyond High Wallowbarrow farm, followed by a glorious stroll over high fell. The way then descends through Dunnerdale Forest to come to the side of the turquoise-coloured River Duddon, which you cross by a footbridge. The return is made through the delightful pastures below the Seathwaite Fells. Well waymarked. Some wet paths after rain.

Map: OS Outdoor Leisure 6.

Nearest towns: Broughton-in-Furness, Ambleside.

Public transport: Post bus from Broughton village, inquiries 01229 716220. North Western Trains, Barrow to Foxfield. Walk to Broughton (1½ miles) to pick up post bus, inquiries 0345 484950.

Refreshments and toilets: Broughton, Ambleside.

Before you set off, cross the road to visit "Wonderful Walker's" church. The Rev Robert Walker was born in 1709 and died in his 93rd year after 67 years as curate of Seathwaite. His starting stipend was £5 a year, his wife brought him a dowry of £40 and after a long life of thrifty habits and persistent industry he left £2000. After his death, he was described as "a man singular for his temperance, industry and integrity". Outside the church porch is a stone he used as a seat when clipping his sheep.

The Walk

Take the signposted footpath opposite the church and go on to pass through a narrow squeeze stile. Walk beside the dancing Tarn Beck to your right and then cross it on a footbridge. The path continues, curving left to cross a small clapper bridge. Stride on the clear path over an open pasture and into birch and hazel woodland. Keep beside a wall to your left and dawdle along the lovely way to cross the narrow walled stone footbridge over the racing River Duddon and into the National Trust's area of Wallowbarrow. Bear left to pass through trees and then go through a gate out onto a pasture. Walk ahead to take a waymarked gate in the far corner.

Pass through another gate and turn right before High Wallowbarrow farm, following the sign for Grassguards. Climb the steadily ascending track through deciduous woodland. Pause here and look back for a good view of Stickle Pike,

Arched bridge, Wallowbarrow

Caw and White Pike. Continue uphill, close under Wallowbarrow Crag, with the chuckling of Rake Beck accompanying you.

Cross the beck on large boulders and continue above the tree-line. Soon the bracken is left behind and the slopes are covered with heather. At a gateless gap in the wall ahead and at a meeting of paths, turn right. The pleasing easy-to-walk track takes you on over the high fell of Rowantree How, where bracken and heather intermingle. Ahead looms the shapely Harter Fell and to the right, across the valley, you can see the quarry on White Pike. As you continue notice the magnificent walling, with huge boulders used along the base.

Then the track descends towards Grassguards farm, which stands guardian to Dunnerdale Forest. Cross the beck by the ford, or use the footbridge, and continue on for a few metres. Turn right before the gate to take the narrow footpath that descends beside the tumbling stream. To your left are dark conifers, but just beyond a gate you pass below some lofty beeches that in autumn are gloriously arrayed in bronze leaves. Descend steadily walking carefully as you

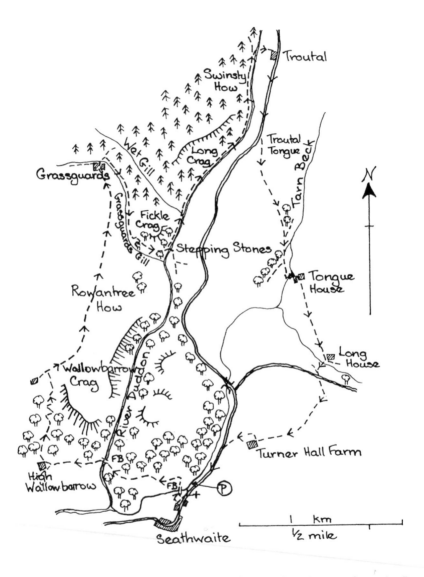

move into the forest over many tree roots that can be slippery after rain. Pass below Fickle Crag to come to the stepping stones over the Duddon. Do not cross, but turn left to walk upstream.

From now on until you reach duck-boarding, the path beside the magnificent Duddon is rough, and muddy after rain, and requires care. Pass the pretty waterfall that plummets out of Wet Gill and continue below Long Crag and

Swinsty How to the splendid footbridge at Troutal. Cross and follow the clear waymarking to the road. Turn right and walk, steadily climbing, enjoying the view over Dunnerdale Forest, the river and the area through which you have just walked.

Cross the cattle grid and walk on for 50 metres to take a signposted footpath going off left. It climbs away from the road and continues ahead, over Troutal Tongue. Continue in the same general direction with a fenced area to your left. Stride on to a corner of the fence and then on to another corner to cross a footbridge. It is in the middle of a wet area – be warned! Then the well walked path becomes dry and leads to a stone stile in the wall. Beyond, dawdle on through the bracken to descend into birch woodland. Follow the path as it swings right. Pass through a gate, and walk in front of a pretty cottage to another gate, which carries a notice asking you to close it. Strike left to a wooden footbridge over Tarn Beck.

Turn left to walk in front of Tongue House farm. Pass through a gate and bear right to go through a difficult-to-spot waymarked gate. Continue ahead over two pastures on the well waymarked route to come to Long House. Turn right and stride the narrow road to a T-junction. Turn left and immediately pass through a signposted gate on your right. Press on to pass to the right of a dwelling named High Moss. Follow its access track in the direction of Turner Hall farm. Beyond the next gate swing right, to avoid the farm, and continue to the next gate onto a metalled track. Walk ahead to the end and turn left to walk down the road to rejoin your car.

Walk 17: Caw

Hawk Bridge – Water Yeat Bridge – Stephenson Ground – Long Mire –
Disused Quarry – Caw – Tail Crag – Natty Bridge – Hawk Bridge

Start/finish: The parking area at Hawk Bridge at the south west corner of Appletreeworth forest (GR 239919) To reach this quiet hollow, beside the Appletree Worth Beck, leave the A593, from Broughton-in-Furness to Coniston, at the turn-off for Broughton Mills. Take the first right turn and then, at the crossroads, continue ahead, dropping downhill to cross the bridge over the beck – the car park lies on your right.

Type of walk: This exciting 6½-miler takes you through a remote corner of the Lickle Valley. The climb to Caw (1,735 ft/529m) requires some scrambling but the views from the summit are breathtaking. The descent to the side of the River Lickle is pathless and from there the path to Natty Bridge is sometimes wet. Beyond, forest roads and paths return you to the car park.

Map: OS Outdoor Leisure 6 (new series).

Nearest village: Broughton-in-Furness, Coniston.

Public transport: Post bus from Broughton, inquiries 01229 716220.

Refreshments and toilets: Broughton, Coniston, Torver.

Caw, together with Stickle Pike and Great Stickle, forms a rugged group of little hills, the Dunnerdale Fells, which lie between the towering heights of Coniston Old Man and the sprawling mass of Black Combe. Caw, the summit of which is the aim of this walk, means Calf, but the fell at 1735ft/529m high is no gentle hill climb. There are few paths and the slopes are steep, the summit being surrounded by innumerable rocky outcrops. And yet there is a good way up to the top, and from it, requiring only a little scrambling.

The Walk

Return to the narrow road and turn right to climb gently for just over half a mile, with the forest to your right. Cross the picturesque stone Water Yeat Bridge. Just beyond, on the right, set into the banking, is a well preserved potash pit. Here bracken was burnt to provide lye, which was later added to tallow to make soap for washing the wool of sheep. Continue on the narrow lane to pass, on your right, two barns, and then go right through the signposted gate beyond.

Stride ahead with the farmhouse, Stephenson Ground, to your left. Keep the wall to your left and quickly join a splendid track. In parts the walls enclosing the track are more than six feet high. Look for the huge boulders used for their footings. At the base of one wall is a fine example of a hogg-hole. Such holes allowed hoggs, year-old sheep, to pass from one pasture to another. This one has a gable top. The hole is blocked with a boulder.

Look for the gaps in the wall where hexagonal "bars" of rock have been used to allow the beck to pass through while preventing sheep from straying onto the track. Go through a gate at the end of the track and bear left to walk a clear

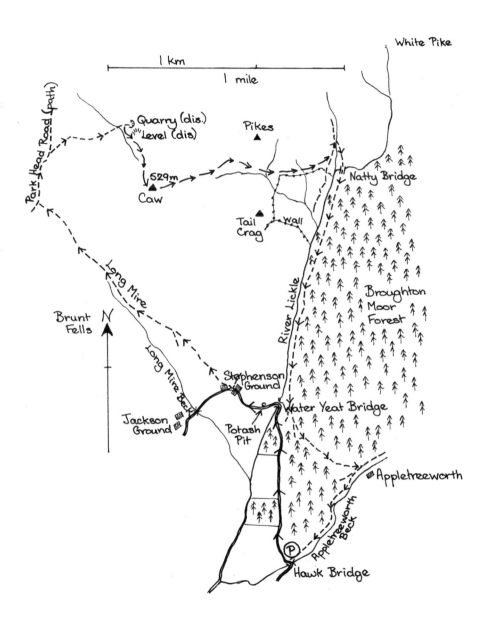

Beck Bars, Long Mire

path beside Long Mire Beck. It takes you, generally dry-shod, across the extensive damp area between Caw and the Brunt Fells, finally passing below the very steep and craggy west face of Caw.

On joining a wide track beside a wall, turn right to walk Park Head Road (a track), once a well used route between the villages of Seathwaite and Broughton Mills. After 450 metres take the grassy track going off right. This is the route to the disused Caw Quarry and is well constructed. Look for the retaining parapet of slate, breached only in one place by a hurrying stream.

After half a mile you reach a huge spoil heap and a ruined hut. Follow the grassy way as it winds right and then left to a flat area in front of another quarry hut. Close by is an adit into the heart of Caw. The entrance is softened with juniper, broom, ferns and liverworts. Do not explore.

Follow an indistinct, occasionally cairned, path to the right of the level. The faint path climbs parallel with a small stream to a junction of clearer narrow paths. Here, with the trig point clearly in view, bear left and follow the path between craggy outcrops to the summit. The magnificent view embraces the tree-girt village of Seathwaite, Harter Fell, Green Crag, the Scafell range, Whit Fell, Devoke Water, the Duddon Estuary, the Hoad at Ulverston, Coniston Water, Morecambe Bay, and Ingleborough.

Leave the summit by a narrow path, heading east-north-east and keeping just to the left (north) of the spine of the ridge. The path becomes less clear as it descends a steepish slope and comes to a wide flat area. Another narrow path takes you across this, avoiding most of the boggy patches.

As you go look for the path climbing the slopes ahead. This leads you up through more rocky outcrops. If you wish to stand by the cairn on the top of Tail Crag, follow a path that bears right. To continue, stroll the main path as it veers left and then winds down, curving slightly right, through the jagged rocks, to another narrow miry plateau, which you cross.

Go on, still east-north-east. The little path weaves round boulders and down over squelchy patches to come to a wall corner. By now you will see the top end of the forest. Descend as close as is convenient to the wall, now on your right, and watch for your first sighting, across the valley, of the wooden bridge that gives access into the forest. The very sketchy path (completely obscured by bracken in summer) brings you down to the side of a small feeder of the River Lickle.

This lovely river rises on the lonely slopes of White Pike. It flows wildly and noisily over its rocky bed, past the huge plantations of the forest and under the wooden bridge. It rages through a tree-lined gorge, before passing under Water Yeat Bridge, crossed earlier. At Hawk Bridge, where you have parked, it unites with Appletree Worth Beck and then hurries on, through Broughton Mills, eventually to add it waters to the River Duddon, below Broughton.

At the side of the narrow stream, walk left for a few yards then step across. Follow a continuing path as it bears right across another wettish area in the direction of the fine wooden footbridge. Take care as you cross – the Lickle seems a long way down and the bridge has no handrail on one side. Once over, look for the abutments of the old packhorse bridge, Natty Bridge, which the wooden bridge has replaced.

Beyond, a short path leads to a sturdy stile into the forest. Stride ahead, for nearly a mile, along the forest ride, with the chattering river away to the right. Then look for the waymark, directing you left into the trees. Follow the narrow path, which is occasionally waymarked and has faint dark blue circles of paint on some trees. It leads you through the forest for three-quarters of a mile to come to a wide ride, where you turn right.

Stroll on towards the car park. As you go look left to see the lonely ruins of Appletree Worth farm, forlorn among the trees on the opposite side of the beck.

Walk 18: Stickle Pike

Hawk Bridge – Lind End Bridge – Carter Ground – Kiln Bank Cross –
Stickle Tarn – Stickle Pike – Park Head Road (track) – Long Mire –
Stephenson Ground – Hawk Bridge

Start/finish: As for walk 17.

Type of walk: An exhilarating 6½-mile walk, which is full of contrasts and takes you through quiet lanes and ancient coppiced woodland, along fellside tracks and up a short rough summit path. You return on a clear path across a lonely stretch of miry fell and through a delightful walled way. Generally easy walking, except for a little scrambling to the Pike.

Map: OS Outdoor Leisure 6 (new series).

Nearest town: Broughton-in-Furness, Coniston. Post bus from Broughton, inquiries 01229 716220.

Refreshments and toilets: Broughton, Torver, Coniston.

From the parking area at Hawk Bridge, walk back over the river and climb the narrow road to the crossroads. Here take the right branch and continue for half a mile along an equally narrow hedged road. Take the stile in the wall on the right, signposted Carter Ground.

Beyond, descend the steep pasture, bearing slightly right, to join a cart track. Turn left before the wall ahead to walk behind Lind End farm, from where you have a good view of its spinning gallery. As the track swings left, continue ahead through a gate, following the footpath sign. Drop down the path, under trees, to the Lind End packhorse bridge, called by some the Fairy Bridge. Below, the River Lickle rages through a steep-sided ravine.

Climb the path, which continues through deciduous woodland. Look left to see a small raised platform, the remains of an old pitstead, once used for producing charcoal from coppiced timber. Leave the woodland by a gate to a field, where you walk ahead to pass through a gap in a wall. Go on to another gateless gap and look for the gate stoop, with the date 1663 and the name Carter carved on it. Stride ahead to a gate into a small larch plantation.

Climb through the trees to a stile, which lies to the right of the path, out onto open pasture. Stride on, keeping to the right of a wall, and continue to a ladder stile to the fell road, which you cross. Go ahead on the reinforced track, signposted Carter Ground, with a small stream to your right. Pass through the gate to the left of a cattle-grid and walk to the left of several attractive dwellings. Continue through a charming garden to a gate to the fell.

Follow the indistinct path that goes ahead to join a wider path, where you turn left. Walk on the pleasing way to pass below Raven's Crag. Here the track divides and you need to take the right fork and go on along the high level path. From here you have a fine view of Stickle Pike, the aim of this walk.

Continue on and then follow the path as it steadily winds left, passing old mining levels and large piles of quarry waste. It takes you to fell road at the brow

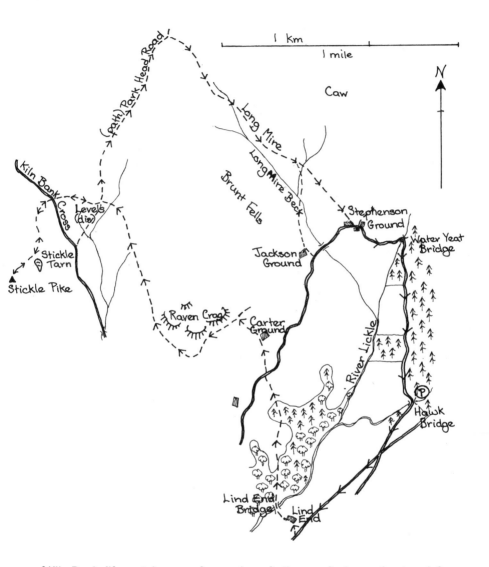

of Kiln Bank. (If you take one of a number of other confusing paths, turn left or right as appropriate to reach the brow.) This narrow road links Broughton Mills with Hall Dunnerdale.

Cross the road and walk ahead for 30 metres along a rising grassy path. Look for a narrower path going off left and follow this as it gradually ascends and comes to the end of the pretty, reedy Stickle Tarn. Bear right here and begin your short steepish ascent to the shapely summit cairn on its wedge of rock.

Stickle Pike

Wander, with care, over the little ridge to a second cairn at the southern end. Pause here and enjoy the view of Bowfell, Scafell, Pillar and the other Coniston fells. To the west the estuary stretches away beyond the lovely Duddon valley.

To return, descend with care to the tarn and then go on down the path to the brow of Kiln Bank Cross. Go over the road and walk ahead along the track you walked earlier, or use one of several paths that lead through the outcrops. They all come together at a wide track, named Park Head Road, once much used by quarry workers for getting to their work and for the removal of slate from the now disused Caw Quarry.

Turn left onto this wider way and walk on over open slopes. The track continues close to a wall on your left. Cross Long Mire Beck on convenient boulders and bear right to leave the main track. (This is the path walked in Walk 17, in the opposite direction, to ascend Caw. At this point you might wish to extend your walk by returning over Caw, adding several more fairly arduous miles to your day.)

To continue, you can take one of several paths that pass below the foot of the craggy west face of Caw. All come together to cross the extensive damp area about Long Mire Beck between Caw and the Brunt Fells. At the junction of the beck with Broadslack Beck, which has cascaded down the slopes of Caw, go on ahead along a delightful wide track, which leads to a gate on the right. Pass through and walk the splendid walled track that leads to Stephenson Ground.

Continue beside the wall on your right to a gate to join the fell road. Turn left and descend steadily to pass the potash pit on the left. Cross Water Yeat Bridge. Walk on along the delightful lane. Once out of the trees on the right, enjoy the pleasing views of the Lickle Valley. Stroll on to the parking area on the right, just before Hawk Bridge.

Walk 19: Duddon Bridge Circular

*Bank End – River Duddon – River Lickle – A595 – River Lickle – Low Moss
– Lower Bleansley – Bleansley Bank – Bank End*

Start/finish: This delightful 2½-miler starts from a lay-by on the right side of the road
to Ulpha, less than 200 metres from Duddon Bridge (GR 199883)

Type of walk: In winter and spring this is a pleasing walk, but once the stinging nettles
and bracken are in full flush, progress becomes difficult along the walled track and up
the slope to Lower Bleansley. The lovely way needs regular use to keep down the
rampant vegetation.

Map: OS Outdoor Leisure 6 (new series).

Nearest towns: Millom, Ulverston, Broughton-in-Furness.

Public transport: Stagecoach Cumberland bus service 7, inquiries 01946 63222.

Refreshments/toilets: Broughton-in-Furness.

---

*The River Duddon rises close to the summit of Wrynose Pass and reaches the sea
after passing through 14 miles of some of the loveliest scenery in Cumbria. After
gathering its waters on the lonely fells it hurries on through pastures and glorious
mixed woodland. It comes close to the village of Seathwaite and then flows*

Duddon Bridge

through the scattered settlement of Ulpha. On it goes past Duddon Hall and then close to the remains of Duddon furnace. It passes under Duddon Bridge before picking up the waters of the River Lickle. Finally it enters its broad estuary and then flows on into the Irish Sea.

From the lay-by, return to cross the busy A-road. Take the track opposite, signposted Lickle Bridge, and follow it as it winds left. The reinforced way is edged by a hedgerow on the left and a copse to the right. Then the track comes close to the surging River Duddon. Go through the signposted gate and keep beside the wall on your left, heading away from the river. Continue on to cross the River Lickle by its tractor bridge.

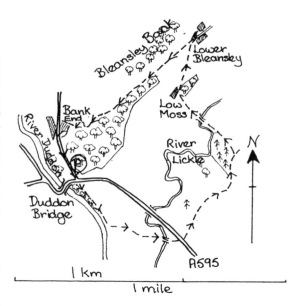

Go on up the hedged track to the side of the A-road once again. Cross, with care, to go through the signposted gate.

Stride on to pass through the gate ahead into a grassy hedged green track. This is the lane that becomes overgrown with nettles and brambles.

Climb a stile and go on, with a plantation to your right. Climb the next stile and walk on, with woodland now to your left. Go through the gate on your left at the edge of the trees. Walk left, beside the woodland, with a fine view, to your right, of the Coniston range of mountains.

Continue on with the River Lickle to your left. Cross the footbridge over the stream and head across the pasture to a gate to Low Moss. Pass through the next gate and wind right in front of the farmhouse to go through a third gate. Carry on towards the outbuildings of Lower Bleansley to go through another gate. Bear left and continue up the slope beside the wall on your right. This is the slope that can be covered in dense bracken, cleavers and stinging nettles. A gate at the end of the wall gives access to a pleasing track. Turn left.

The way ascends gently, with oak woodland beyond the wall to your left. Enjoy this glorious high-level track. After another climb, pass through a gate and then begin your descent to the Ulpha road. Turn left to walk the short distance to the lay-by.

Walk 20: Broughton-in-Furness – Woodland

Broughton – Wall End farm – Thornthwaite Latter Rigg – Woodland Hall – Spunham – Green Moor farm – Woodland church – Buttstead Wood – Mireside farm – East Park – Broughton

Start/finish: Broughton-in-Furness Square (GR 213876) To reach the village take the A5092, at Greenodd, in the direction of Workington. After 7½ miles, watch for the signposted right turn for Broughton.

Type of walk: A fine 8-mile walk for all the family through pleasing countryside. There is a small hill to climb, some fell walking, a tramp through woodland, a stretch along a quiet road and two small streams to cross.

Map: OS Outdoor Leisure 6 (new series).

Nearest town: Ulverston, Broughton-in-Furness.

Public transport: North Western Trains from Barrow or Millom, alight (request) at Foxfield, one mile walk to Broughton Square, inquiries 0345 484950. School buses from Ulverston or Millom, Stagecoach Cumberland, inquiries 01946 63222.

Refreshments/toilets: Broughton.

Broughton lies within the Lake District National Park. In Elizabethan times, it was granted a charter to hold fairs, and it once had a busy woollen trade. The square is surrounded by town houses built in Georgian times. Several large trees shade fish slabs and stocks and there is an obelisk erected for George III's jubilee in 1810.

The Walk

Leave the square by the north-east corner, passing the public toilets. Follow the walled track as it turns right and continue to cross the former railway track. Climb the steps beyond and turn left to follow the waymark. Go through a gateless gap to the next boundary wall, before which you turn right. Continue on to pass through two squeeze stiles. Turn left and go up a slope, through shrubs. Then scramble down the other side to a stile to the Wall End farm access track.

Cross and take another track swinging right, and then left, to descend through glorious woodland. Continue on to emerge onto a narrow lane. Turn left and after 200 metres take the stile on the right, signposted Woodland Hall. Walk ahead, with the wall to your right. Cross a tractor bridge and, beyond the gate, stride the pasture to cross over Kirkby Pool by its stiled bridge.

The way continues ahead – but there is a waymarked diversion if the pasture is wet. Climb straight up the lower slope of Thornthwaite Latter Rigg. Where the path divides take the right branch. At the ridge, turn left to reach the cairn and to enjoy the magnificent view. Go on in the same direction to descend. Aim for a stone-stepped stile to the left of a gate. Beyond go on to join the cart track to Woodland Hall and farm.

Turn right through the gate to walk between the farm buildings. Follow the track as it bears right and then left and winds gently downhill through delightful

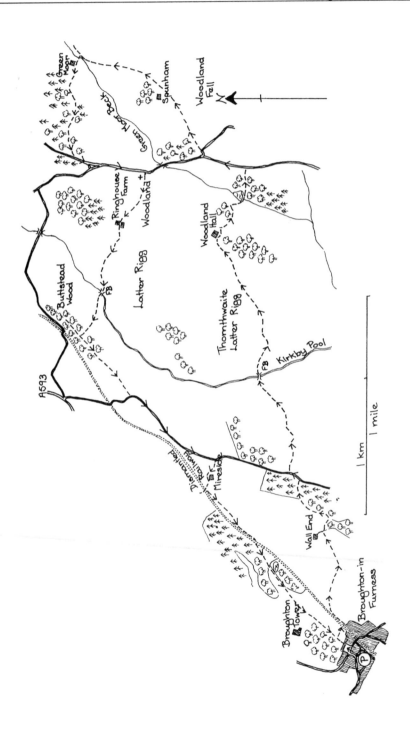

countryside to join a moorland road. Turn left and walk for 500 metres. At the junction of roads, take the signposted bridleway to continue ahead on the bracken-clad moor. Stride the partly metalled track and then go along the signposted track directing you away from the nearby farm.

Stroll on, keeping parallel with, on the left, the wall and then woodland. Where the trees end, cross a tiny stream and look for a narrow track going off left – very easy to miss when the bracken is fully grown. Follow this pleasing path as it descends towards a small cottage, Green Moor, which lies in a grassy hollow and beyond a clapper bridge.

Cross the exquisite bridge and walk ahead through gates to pass to the left of the cottage. Join its access track and follow it as it descends slightly into Green Moor Wood. Follow the track through the woodland to come to a metalled road. Walk left and continue left of a small island in the road, which is rich in wild flowers. Go on left to walk the narrow road. You are now in the heart of Woodland, a broad valley with scattered dwellings, hemmed in by the Woodland fells, a ridge of Broughton Moor and Torver High Common.

Pass Woodland church and, just beyond, take the signposted right turn to walk to Ringhouse farm. Follow the signpost directions, passing between the buildings and the house. Stride on the clearly arrowed way out onto the rough open pasture of Latter Rigg. There are many tracks here but gradually begin to descend (right) to come close to the beck. Stroll the path as it swings left, until you reach a stile on the right, beyond which lies the bridge over the Kirkby Pool.

Once across, stroll ahead, with the hedge to your left. Cross a tractor bridge, which takes you through the left corner of the hedge ahead. Go on, still with the hedge to your left, and continue towards Buttstead Wood. Pass through a narrow gap stile on the left, turn right and enter the wood by a sturdy wooden stile. Walk through the trees and turn left on joining the main path. This is a glorious piece of ancient woodland full of flowers and birdsong.

Leave the wood by a gate and walk ahead along the path, and then a track bordered with hedgerow trees, until the Five Arches Road is attained. Continue onwards to Mireside farm. Turn right, passing between the farmhouse and the outbuildings. Climb the track beyond and, just before the disused railway track; take the stile on the left.

Walk ahead to pass through a gate in the wall. Continue ahead, by the wall and hedge. Look for the easy-to-miss "fat man's agony" stile on the right, set in the hedgerow. Pass through, turn left and walk diagonally right over a hillock to a gate close to the old railway track. Walk on by the hedge on your right and take the stepped stile in the hedgerow on the right. This gives access to the disused railway, which you cross, and climb up steps on the opposite side.

Turn left and walk diagonally right to a kissing gate. Beyond, go ahead, with Broughton's two pleasing lakes to your left. Head towards Broughton Tower, keeping to the left of it, to a kissing gate into a copse. Walk ahead to pass out of the trees. Go by the village swings and roundabouts. Saunter on to a walled track and continue ahead into Broughton's square.

Walk 21: Broughton-in-Furness — Aulthurst Side

Broughton Square – Dismantled railway – Mireside – Old School House – West Park – Broughton.

Start/finish: Broughton Square (GR 213876). To reach the village take the A5092, at Greenodd, in the direction of Workington. After 7½ miles, watch for the signposted right turn for Broughton.

Type of walk: This 3½-mile walk takes you along the quiet dismantled railway, where you might like to pause by two small lakes. Then, by pastures and walled paths, it brings you to the old schoolhouse. The return is made over pleasing pastures and through woodland.

Map: OS Outdoor Leisure 6, The English Lakes, south western area (new series).

Nearest towns: Ulverston, Millom.

Public transport: North Western Trains from Barrow or Millom, alight (request) at Foxfield, one-mile walk to Broughton Square, inquiries 0345 484950. School buses from Ulverston or Millom, Stagecoach Cumberland, inquiries 01946 63222.

Refreshments and toilets: Broughton.

On this walk you might spot the top of Broughton Tower rising above the many trees in its grounds. It looks romantic and mysterious and was once the seat of the Broughton family. It was taken away from them by Henry VII after Sir Thomas Broughton, unwisely, supported Lambert Simnel's unsuccessful attempt to seize the throne and have himself crowned as the rightful king (see walk 30).

In 1859 Coniston village was linked by rail to Foxfield, the trains passing through Broughton. This enabled large quantities of slate quarried in the fells to be carried away for processing. In 1958 this delightful line, which also carried goods, tourists, schoolchildren and many passengers, passing through delectable countryside, was closed by Dr Beeching.

The Walk

Leave the square by the north-east corner, passing the toilets. Follow the walled way as it turns right and continue to the side of the track of the former railway. Turn left. Go through the cutting, where the exposed rock supports a variety of ferns. In spring wild daffodils and then bluebells brighten the way. Pass under an old bridge,

Daffodils

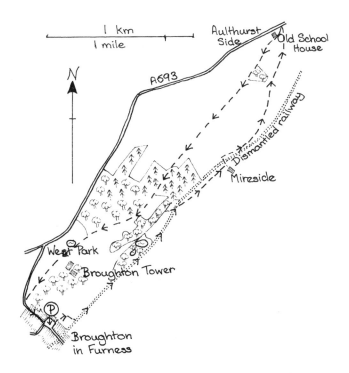

heavy with ivy and, a short distance along, climb the low banking on the left to sit on the seat and enjoy the lovely lakes. Here you might see coots, mallards, tufted duck, dabchicks and great crested grebes.

Rejoin the railway and stroll on to pass gates on the left and right. Then, a few metres on, look for a row of steps on both sides of the track. Climb those on your right. Once in a pasture, continue on in the same general direction to pass through a gate with an awkward catch. Continue over a small hillock and then drop right to pass through a narrow squeeze stile, often called "a fat man's agony".

Press on beside the hedge on your left to pass through a gate and then beside a pool to a stile to a track. Turn left and go between the buttresses of another bridge. Pass a drinking trough on your left.

Just beyond take a narrow hedged track that starts just after a field gate on the left. Climb steadily to come to the side of a small copse of oak. Where the trees end, climb a stile into a wider walled track. Stride the lovely way. Step across a small stream and straddle a further stile. Beyond, the path bears slightly right and takes you through a variety of colourful vegetation. Pause here to enjoy the view down into Woodland. This is the haunt of goldcrests and long tailed tits.

Go over the next stile and follow the track as it swings left. Just before the road turn left to walk the drive of the old schoolhouse, now a private dwelling, and follow the arrowed way, left and then right, along the edge of the lawn to come to a stone step stile in the far wall.

Continue on beside the wall on your left to climb the next step stile. Stroll beside more oak woodland, to your left, and follow the narrow path that takes you over small streams and through a gap in the hedge. Dawdle on, beside the hedge and wall on your right, with a glorious view ahead. Look for the next stile, up against the hedge, top right corner.

Walk ahead and then you may need to make a detour through gaps in the hedge on the right to avoid an often-wet area about another small stream. Once beyond this, return through the hedge to take a stone step stile ahead. Walk on with the hedge now to your left.

Go through the unusual revolving metal stile into woodland and descend the delightful track, where you might spot roe deer – or just their white rumps as they race away. Emerge from the trees by a stile into a pasture, with conifers to your right. Walk ahead through a gateless gap and go on, with more conifers to your right, to take a kissing gate to the left of a gate.

Beyond, notice the interesting stile to your left, with its wheel-shaped handrail. Ignore this and descend to climb a similar stile, which takes you into West Park. Stroll across this large pasture to a hand gate to the road, in the far right corner. Cross the road with care and bear left to round a blind corner – again with utmost care. Continue on to descend the road to return to Broughton Square.

Stocks and fish slab, Broughton

Walk 22: Angerton and Thornthwaite Latter Rigg

Broughton-in-Furness – Coal Gate – Foxfield – Waitham Hill – Chapels – Grizebeck – Far Houses – Woodland Hall – Thornthwaite Latter Rigg – Kirkby Pool – Wall End – Broughton-in-Furness.

Start/finish: Village Square, Broughton-in-Furness (GR 213876).

Type of walk: This 10-mile walk, the longest in the book, takes you through the quiet, delightful countryside close to the estuary and then inland through the pleasing pastures, woodlands and low fells about Woodland. Much of the way is level walking, with one short scramble up Thornthwaite Latter Rigg. By completing this long route, road walking is kept to a minimum.

Map: OS Outdoor Leisure 6 (new series).

Nearest town: Broughton.

Public transport: See walk 20.

Refreshments and toilets: Broughton.

Leave Broughton Square by walking south-east – that is, on the road that passes the Manor Arms public house to your left. Descend the hill. Cross two roads and climb the steepish hill ahead, almost to the brow. Opposite the entrance to the primary school (the school buildings are hidden from view), turn right into a pleasing narrow hedged lane.

As you go enjoy extensive views over Broughton, with its church, to Black Combe, sitting solidly and imposing at the end of the chain of lesser fells. Continue past a dwelling house on the left and then another on the right named Dower House, and go on to Miller's Cottage, directly in front of you. Take the sometimes muddy path through a copse to the left of the cottage.

Go through a gap in the railings, once part of a kissing gate and, with care, head across the fine turf of the golf links, which may be in use. Pass a waymarked post for the Cum-

Primroses and wood sorrel

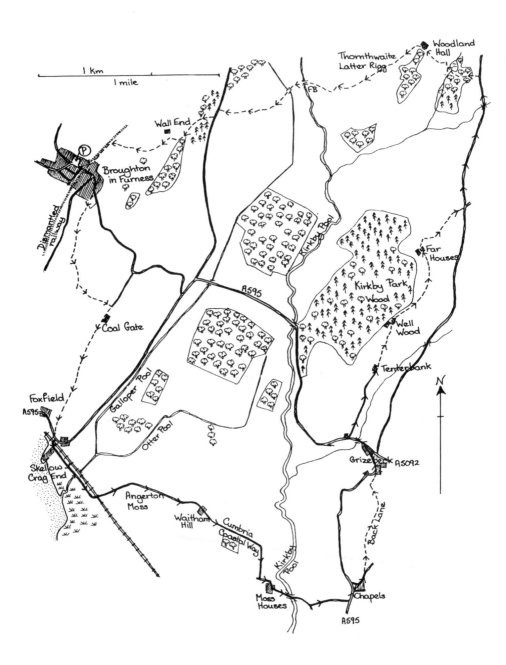

bria Coastal Way (CCW) and descend a gentle slope to pass another CCW marker. Head slightly right to cross a footbridge over a small stream. Beyond, strike uphill to pass through a wall. Go on uphill through two pastures to join a narrow road. Turn right to walk between the dwellings of Coal Gate. Descend, gently, to the A595 Cross with care and go on, slightly left, to go over the railway track, turning left on the far side.

Follow the road (CCW) that continues along beside the railway track, with Skellow Crag and then saltmarsh vegetation to the right. Where the road swings right towards Angerton, turn left and re-cross the railway line. Continue on this virtually traffic-free secluded way, which is bordered with birch, rowan and gorse, and follow it as it swings across marshland.

Go on past the farm at Waitham Hill and continue on the metalled road. At a T-junction, turn left to Moss Houses. Very shortly the metalling ceases. Cross the bridge over the Kirkby Pool and go ahead, ignoring left and right turns. As the track veers right, go ahead to take, on the left (Cumbria Cycle Way), a hedged lane which leads you back to the A595. Cross with care and walk left to take the second right turn. Stride up the narrow lane, behind the houses of the hamlet of Chapels, to take the signposted track on the left, named Back Lane.

Press on along this attractive way as it climbs between low hedges. In spring the banks are bright with bluebells, primroses, wood sorrel and wood anemone. The lane gradually descends to Grizebeck village. At the road, continue ahead to cross the A-road again.

Turn left and walk past several houses and a boat repairers to ascend on the right, just before the old school, a reinforced right of way which continues through Tenter Bank farm. Continue along a signposted grassy way, and beside a wall on your left, to a gate. Beyond, follow the track through derelict buildings and go with it as it swings right. Stride the walled track beside Kirkby Park Wood. Where the wood ends, continue ahead to a gate, which gives access to another walled track.

Descend the gated and stiled track, with ahead a splendid view of the Coniston fells. Pass through Far Houses farm buildings, also derelict. Go on along a frequently muddy track and walk on to a metal gate in the wall on the right, through which you pass. Go on through two more gates by a dwelling and walk on to cross a cattle grid to a reinforced lane. Bear right to the crossroads.

Turn left and walk the delightful way to take a left turn, signposted Woodland Hall. (The following route has been walked in the reverse direction in walk 20.) Stride ahead through deciduous woodland. Notice the small lake on the right surrounded with banks of rhododendrons – a mass of pink blossoms in May. Continue uphill. Follow the track as it winds left, and then right, past dwellings and outbuildings, to a gate ahead onto the open fell. Beyond bear left.

After 150 metres leave the track to take another branching right. Follow this to the wall ahead and climb it using the through-steps or go through the gate if open. Climb the gently rising slopes of Thornthwaite Latter Rigg to the cairn (295ft/90m). Pause here and enjoy the grand panoramic view. Stroll on the continuing little ridge and then, towards the end, take a path that leaves left and then winds round right to a waymark at the foot of the fell.

Go on (west) over the pasture, following the waymarks (there are two routes, one for when the ground is wet) to a sturdy footbridge over Kirkby Pool. Stride ahead over an often wettish pasture to a gate and a clapper bridge over a drainage ditch.

Carry on ahead along the clear track over rough pasture that keeps beside a wall on your left. All through the summer this area is gloriously colourful, with a variety of flowers. Continue to a signposted stile to the road. Turn left and after, 20 metres, turn right into a wide track through beech and sycamore woodland where foxgloves flower on the track side.

Follow the wide track as it climbs steeply through trees and, where the way divides, take the right fork for a few paces to a farm access track. Cross and climb the stile opposite and go up the bank beyond. Walk on along one of several tracks, keeping parallel with the wall to your right. Continue to a narrow gap stile (a fat man's agony), which lies just beyond the first wall going off right.

Pass through and walk beside the wall, now on your right, to the next even narrower gap stile. Beyond strike diagonally left, across two pastures. In the far corner take the stone steps to the bed of a disused railway. Turn left down the track and, at the road, turn right and walk uphill to Broughton Square.

Walk 23: Great Burney Fell – Beacon Tarn

Burney – Great Burney – Little Burney – Crooked Birch – Tottlebank –
Cockenskell – Beacon Tarn – Wool Knott – High Kep – Blawith Knott –
Giant's Grave – Settlement – Heathwaite Gate – Heathwaite Farm – Knott
End – Knittleton – Burney Tarn

Start/finish: A lay-by on the west side of the narrow road that leaves north, off the A5092 (GR 262849). The reinforced lay-by (GR 259852) is found ¼ of a mile along the road at the foot of Great Burney fell.

Type of walk: A very satisfying 8-mile round of small summits with a peep at Beacon Tarn and a pause at the Giant's Grave, and a Romano-British settlement beside a gullery. The footpaths are well waymarked but once you are on the fell there are many sheep trods and few clear paths. Fortunately you can look ahead from the low tops to see the general direction in which you need to continue, and the views are spectacular too.

Map: OS Outdoor Leisure 6 (new series).

Nearest town: Ulverston.

Public transport: North Western Train to Askam, inquiries 034 484959. Bus 509, Askam, Kirkby, Grizebeck, Gawthwaite, Ulverston, inquiries Stagecoach Cumberland 01946 63222.

Refreshments/toilets: Broughton-in-Furness, Ulverston, Grizebeck garage.

Cross the fell road and begin your ascent of Great Burney by bearing left up a rather indistinct path. At what appears to be the brow, a wide grassy track continues over a flatter area, and then climbs to the trig point. Pause here for a wonderful view of the estuary and the long stretch of the Furness Fells from Black Combe to Wetherlam. Beyond you can glimpse the Scafells. To the north east you can see Helvellyn, Fairfield and Ill Bell, with lesser heights between. To your left you can peep into the Duddon valley and to the right that of the Crake.

Look down into the valley immediately ahead to see a fine white farmhouse – Birch Bank. To its right, and nearer to you, lies difficult-to-spot Little Burney, a small rise from the north ridge of Great Burney beyond the narrow stretch of moor known as Grey Stone Moss. Head towards the subsidiary fell; leaving the trig point to the right and edging round the moss. A good path skirts the left side of the small fell. When you have located this, leave it soon to attain the tiny summit and then rejoin the path again. Walk right to come near to a wall, with mixed woodland beyond. Continue downhill to join a gated narrow road, where you turn right.

At the access track (50 metres) to Crooked Birch farm, leave the road and walk left, to pass right of the dwelling. Walk left through the farmyard to take a small waymarked gate. Look for Tottlebank farm high up on the slopes above the valley; this is where you are heading next.

Beyond the gate, walk ahead over the pasture to climb a stile and go on down to a footbridge in the bottom right corner – it stands beside a telegraph

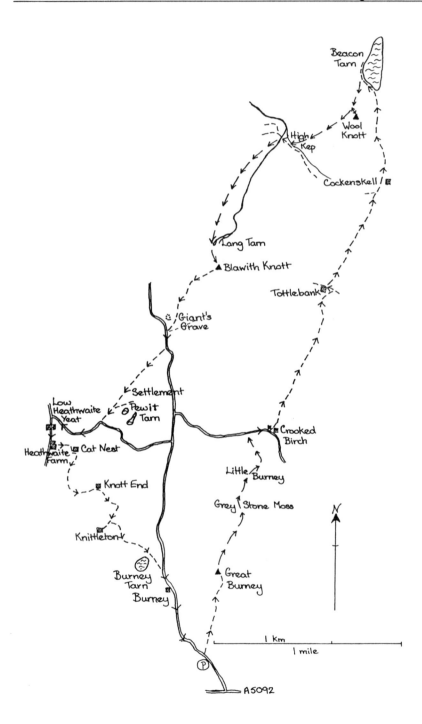

pole. Cross a wet area and bear slightly right (picking the driest way after rain), to a kissing gate near to the wall that has come in on your left. Cross a turf bridge and climb steadily up the steep slope, with a beck to your right and the farmhouse to your left. Go through the farm gate in the wall ahead; bear right along the farm access track to a gate to a narrow road.

Turn right and after 20 metres take the signposted footpath swinging left up onto pleasing fell. Enjoy this delightful way over the slopes, which brings you to a gate close to a dwelling named Cockenskell away to your right. Stride the walled way and after the next gate follow the shelf-like path that bears right and then left, winding downhill through trees to a grass bridge over the beck.

Follow the continuing path that climbs steadily and clearly, beside a wall to your left and through bracken fell with scattered holly and juniper. Go on over the brow, with a great view ahead of Dow Crag and the Old Man awaiting you. Descend towards the lovely Beacon Tarn. Bear left and after 50 metres bear left again to ascend a green path through the heather. It passes close to the foot of Wool Knott, to your left. Climb easily, left, to find a comfortable rock seat on the summit for your picnic.

Leave your perch on the top and return to the green path. Turn left and stroll on, the path leading away from the tarn. Stride on over the slopes, with Black Combe coming into view. Continue down to a permanently wet area, with a small cairn, to join a wide track coming up from Cockenskell. This is named High Kep on the OS map. Turn left and after 10 steps turn right to take a green path climbing the slope, keeping to the west (right) side of Mere Sike. Continue on the narrow but distinct path edging outcrops to the right. Go on through a quiet hollow surrounded by rocky hillocks to Lang Tarn, which is fed by a spring. It is considered the smallest tarn in Lakeland.

Beyond the tarn take any narrow path climbing up left to Blawith Knott, with its three scattered cairns. Enjoy the magnificent view. Leave the summit by a wide green trod in the direction of the estuary. Avoid the first path off left and descend by the gently dropping green trod that takes you easily down the slopes to a short stretch of grassy track and then the narrow fell road. At this spot look for a long barrow, possibly Bronze Age, named as Giant's Grave on the OS map. It has a large stone at its head and a smaller one at the foot. Once there might have been a double row

Giant's Grave

of stones edging the 2-metre long hollow. Legend has it that one of a family of huge men, who lived nearby, was buried here.

On joining the road, turn left and, ignoring the signposted footpaths, walk on for 150 metres to take a wide grassy track going off on the right, just before a hillock. Keep to the left branch, where the path divides and, just beyond, look left to see the remains of prehistoric huts and enclosures, possibly iron-age, set around Pewit tarn and several other small pools. Here in early summer gregarious black-headed gulls nest on mats of sticks, sedges or rushes, raised above the level of the water and there is a constant noise as the birds scold and screech.

Go on along the track to descend to the narrow road. Turn right and walk downhill to the crossroads at Fell Gate. Turn left and walk to Heathwaite Farm, where you turn left again, following the signpost for Knott End. Walk ahead through the outbuildings to a gate onto pasture. Walk uphill to the hedge and turn right to stroll to a waymark. This directs you in front of a barn and then to the side of a dwelling called Cat Nest. Beyond the gate walk left to a hedged track and continue along it.

Climb the stile; follow the track as it curves left to pass through gate onto fell. The slopes to your left, at the right time of the year, are a blaze of yellow gorse and the air is heavily perfumed. Stride on to a stile in the fence on the right. Beyond carry on, descending steadily to a step stile in the bottom right corner.

Go with a wall to your right to a gateway, just before a pink house. Keep right of the charming dwelling and follow the access track to cross a cattle grid and then the beck. Immediately turn right to walk up beside the wall to join another track, where you turn right to press on towards the farm of Knittleton.

Before the cattle grid to the farm, turn left and climb a wide grassy track. This bears left and then right. Near the brow, and before the next curve, walk ahead on a narrow path, which keeps to the right of a large outcrop, soon to come near Burney Tarn. The water of the tarn is almost lost to sight; its edges colonised with tall reeds. The narrow path takes you between several small pools and leads you to the fell road. Turn right and walk on to rejoin your car. If you fail to find the narrow path, the good track leads you to the road, where you turn right – but you have more tarmac to walk.

NB If you must shorten the walk because of times of trains or buses; turn left beyond Tottlebank farm to walk the cart track. Where it joins the fell road, turn right to see the Giant's Grave and then left to stride up the road (see text) to continue the walk.

Walk 24: Beckside – Kirkby-in-Furness

Beckside – Gill End – High Bank farm – Long Slack Moss – Dalton Moor – Harlock – Gunson Heights – Low Gill House – Beckside.

Start/finish: The parking area beside the Community Centre, Beckside (GR 234823). To reach Beckside turn east off the A595 at Four Lane Ends, Kirkby-in-Furness.

Type of walk: This superb 5-miler passes through pleasing pastures and over rolling heather moorland from where the views are magnificent. There is a long climb to the ridge but this is eased by the zigzags of the old track. Except for one short stretch of moorland, the way is clearly waymarked.

Map: OS Outdoor Leisure 6 (new series).

Nearest towns: Ulverston, Barrow.

Public transport: North Western Trains, inquiries 0345 484950. Postbus 523 Cumberland 7/X7, inquiries 01946 63222.

Refreshments: Kirkby.

Toilets: In car park.

Turn right out of the parking area and walk the narrow lane through the delightful hamlet of Beckside. Visit the parish church of St Cuthbert, where you enter through the well preserved Norman door.

The church dates from the 12th century and has been added to and refurbished several times. Look for the ancient parish chests, cut out of solid blocks of timber, which are possibly older than the church itself. The church has some attractive stained glass and near the pulpit is a 13th century red sandstone tombstone, possibly that of an Abbot of Furness.

Walk on to pass the old school. Turn right in front of Beckside Mill, a working mill until the 1940s, and now a private house. Look for the magnificent waterwheel, the tiny waterfall and the charming garden. Continue along the quiet lane to where it swings left and take the unmarked gate on the right. Beyond, walk the wide gated track to Low Hall farm, enjoying the grand views as you go. Bear right, then left to go on along the metalled access track, with the farmhouse to your left as you proceed. At the lane, turn left.

Stroll the shady way to pass Gill End, with its pretty beck and cascade. Then climb up the hedged lane to High Bank House farm. Pass through the gate on the right, with the farmhouse ahead. Bear slightly right to the clearly waymarked gate. Beyond, continue with the wall and then the fence to your left, just below a house. Pass through a gate and go on parallel with a wall to your right. Beneath a sturdy elm, join a zigzagging track on which you first walk ahead before swinging acute left.

Pass through a derelict wall and go on steadily ascending, following the track to where it curves sharply right. At the wall ahead continue upwards, the steepest part of the walk, taking lots of pauses to enjoy the ever-increasing views of the estuary and the Lakeland Hills. Just before the fell gate look for the

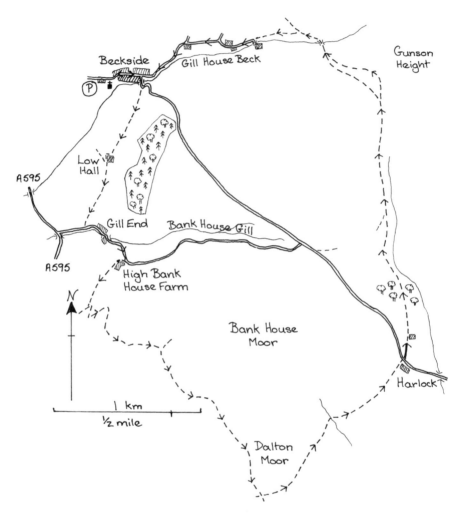

short row of notched stone flags, used as fencing for an old sheep fold. Once through the gate, walk right over the moor, where bilberry predominates and there is a scattering of heather. Here you often see a pair of kestrels hunting for prey.

After 400 metres, and well before the deep groove of Long Slack Beck, look for a narrow, indistinct path bearing off left through the now predominating heather. The path continues parallel with the groove, which lies away to your right. Cross two tiny streams and look ahead to see the path – now a clear way edged with grass and bilberry against the dark colouring of the heather – climbing gently to the right. Once you are over the brow of the moor a distinct path emerges and you can see the green pastures about Harlock reservoir. Pass through the waymarked gate in the boundary fence.

Bear right and descend the slope to join a cart track, where you turn left. This easy way begins to swing north, with great views of Ingleborough and the Howgills. Below, to your right, is the reservoir. Continue on in the direction of a sturdy yellow-topped post by a gate. Beyond the gate, walk ahead on a good gated track towards a house in the valley bottom. The track leads to a gate to the road, to the left of Harlock farm.

Turn right for two or three steps and then cross the road to take the continuing narrow track. Pass through the gate and stroll on along the track to go by a stand of fine beech trees. Beyond the fell gate stride the superb track towards the next yellow-topped post. Walk on as the way bears right and ascends gradually over heather moorland. Soon you can count the 12 windmills used for generating power. Beyond is a dramatic view of the Coniston range of hills.

Where the track divides take the left branch. As it begins to descend, with a sturdy wall to the left, you can again glimpse the estuary. Cross a deepish grassy gill, through which tumbles Gill House Beck, and continue on the wide track towards another marker post.

At this post, turn left and carry on down to cross a feeder stream, about which is a good exposure of Silurian slate. Walk on along an old track to pass through a gate into woodland, with a waymark ahead. Walk on to join a lane. Press on down the narrow way, with high hedges on both sides and a very deep gill to your left. At the T-junction, turn left and stride on downhill. Look left to see more notched flags used as walling. The lane leads you downhill, past the mill, the old school and the church to regain your car.

Kestrel hunting

Walk 25: Dunnerholme

Ireleth – Dunnerholme – Marsh Grange – Pear Tree Beck footbridge – Cross Beck footbridge – Gargreave farm – Dalton Moor – Moor Road – Ireleth.

Start/finish: Parking area in large lay-by on the west side of the A595, just north of St Peter's School, Ireleth (GR 224777).

Type of walk: This pleasing 7-miler takes you, first, over the marsh following waymarked posts, and then the golf course, to Dunnerholme, the large dramatic outcrop of limestone which stands guard over the Duddon Sands. After you cross an area that can be wet after rain, the character of the walk changes as you begin your ascent to the path through heather on Dalton Moor. From then on quiet lanes return you to Ireleth.

Map: OS Outdoor Leisure 6 (new series).

Nearest town: Barrow, Ulverston.

Public transport: Stagecoach Cumberland buses from Barrow via Dalton bypass to Ireleth, inquiries 01946 63222. North Western Trains, Barrow to Askam, inquiries 0345 484950.

Refreshments and toilets: Inns and shops at Askam and Kirkby-in-Furness.

From the parking area walk south towards the village of Ireleth to take the signposted footpath on the right, opposite the school. Drop down the steep reinforced path, cross a small beck on a footbridge and follow the path as it swings left to join Saves Lane. Turn right and walk between the houses. Ignore the first footpath sign and, where the tarmac ends, take the footpath on the right, signposted Dunnerholme.

Tall posts, the tops painted bright yellow, mark the continuing footpath. To the left, low sand-dunes edge the blue water of the estuary and to the right sheep graze the pastures. Keep ahead, bearing very slightly left. Ignore more waymarked posts coming in from the east.

Continue in the same general direction to cross first a tractor bridge and then, with care, the North Western train line. Turn right and, observing a warning about golf balls, follow the waymarked posts over the golf links to join a wide grassy track, between gorse bushes. This is the bed of an old railway that carried lime from Dunnerholme to an ironworks.

Stride on to pass to the right of the picturesque mound and a row of delightful cottages. In these once lived cocklers who supplied their catch to Furness Abbey and also sold them on Dalton market. Turn left beyond the pretty dwellings and walk on along the shore, with Mere Beck flowing fast to the right. Look for two lime kilns built into the side of the cliffs of the huge mound. Sit on the seat and enjoy (depending on the tide) the extensive sands or the surging sea. It is a good place for watching curlews, dunlin and oyster catchers feeding on the water's edge.

Return towards the front of the cottages and take the reinforced track, right,

Lakeland fells from Dunnerholme

to the top of the holme. Here in the hollows, where limestone was removed, sheep now feed on rich grass. From the steep cliffs you can enjoy the magnificent view of the estuary, but take care as you approach the edge.

Leave the mound by the track and continue past the cottages. Carry on inland along the access track to cross the railway line once more. Continue to Marsh Grange farm, a medieval dwelling with four square chimneys. Margaret Askew was born here in 1614. She married Thomas Fell in 1632 and afterwards, in 1669, George Fox, founder of the Society of Friends (Quakers).

Turn left before the farmhouse to walk a track between outbuildings and on through an archway in a wall. Head slightly left to cross the pasture to a stile. Continue ahead along a track to pass a farm called The Guards (1769). Stride on but leave the track where it swings sharp left and pass through a gate ahead. Cross two stiled pastures and then bear diagonally right to a tractor bridge over Pear Tree beck.

Stroll on ahead over a pasture to cross another tractor bridge. Carry on to the right corner and pass through a gate on your right. Continue beside the hedge on your left. Ignore the footbridge over Cross Beck. Pass through the gate ahead and walk on. Ignore the tractor bridge on your left and, beyond, take the gate also on the left, just beyond where the beck makes a dog-leg turn. Bear right across the pasture to where it narrows to join a walled track leading to the A595, which you cross.

Head along the access track to Gargreave farm and pass through the gate to the slopes below Bank House Moor. Climb ahead over the pasture to a gate. Beyond, walk left to follow the pleasant zigzagging path up the steepish slopes. (The next mile of this walk follows the same route as walk 24) Enjoy the magnificent unfolding views of the Furness Fells, the estuary with every channel and gutter visible, and Hodbarrow nature reserve and the sea beyond.

Just before passing through the gate in the wall, bordering the moor, look for a remnant of "fence" made of interlocking Brathay flags. Beyond the gate

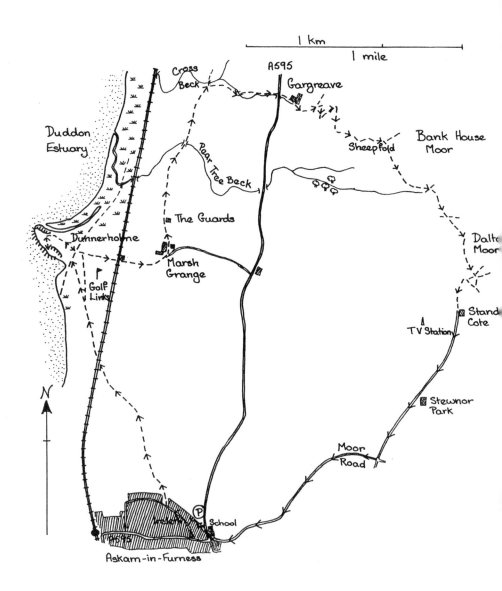

follow the continuing track, a wide grassy swathe that swings right through low-growing heather, the haunt of grouse and snipe.

After 400 metres, and well before the deep groove of Long Slack Beck, leave the good track by a narrow path, left, to walk the indistinct way over the vast heather moorland. Cross two tiny streams and look ahead to see the path – now a clear way edged with grass, which appears very green against the dark heather – climbing gently to the right.

Once you are over the brow of the moor, the green pastures about Harlock reservoir come into view. Pass through the waymarked gate in the boundary fence, just before it joins a wall.

Bear right, dropping down the slope. Join the cart track at the bottom and turn right, following it as it winds left. Stride on where it becomes metalled to pass the dwelling of Standish Cote, the access track to the TV station, and then Stewnor Park. Away to the left stretches Poaka reservoir.

At the crossroads, turn right to walk downhill towards Ireleth. As you stroll down the lovely lane, look left to see several large ponds, where iron-ore was extracted. On reaching St Peter's School, turn right to rejoin your car.

Walk 26: Askam–in-Furness

Askam – Askam Pier – Sand dunes of Sandscale Haws – Lowsy Point –
Sandscale farm – Roanhead – Askam

Start/finish: Small car park on low cliffs, north end of Askam. After crossing the railway line, and where the main road swings left, take the road that leads off right. Continue to the end to park on the left (GR 210780)

Type of walk: A breezy 7½-miler along Askam Sands and edging the sand dunes of
Sandscale Haws. The walk continues through the small settlement at Lowsy Point
and skirts Scarth Bight. The return is along a wide track through pastures, returning to
the shore at Roanhead. There are no hills to climb and the sands are a delight BUT
this walk can be done only when the tide is out for the whole day. When the tide does
turn it races over the estuarine sand at great speed and then a retreat has to be made
into the sand dunes. If on your return you have misjudged the timing, you will not be
able to get round Roanhead Crag. It might be possible, after gaining permission of the
farmer at Roanhead Farm, to use his track to join a narrow road to return to Askam
BUT this is not a right of way.

Map: OS Outdoor Leisure 6 (new series).

Nearest town: Dalton-in-Furness.

Public transport: North Western trains to Askam, inquiries 0345 484950. Stagecoach Cumberland buses, inquiries 01946 63222.

Refreshments: In Askam.

Toilets: At car park and station.

---

*Askam-in-Furness adjoins the village of Ireleth. When, in 1857, a huge reserve of
iron-ore was discovered at Ireleth, long rows of terraced houses were built at
Askam to accommodate the workers of the ironworks. Within ten years the population had risen from 400 to 3,000. Smelting by the Furness Iron and Steel Com-
pany began in 1867. By 1919, when the ore was worked out, the ironworks
closed.*

The Walk

Descend to the shore, from the car park, using the steps nearer the narrow
road. The original flight has been eroded by the tide and, though a few steps remain, the slope is difficult. Once you have enjoyed the glorious view across the
estuary to Millom, Haverigg, Black Combe and White Combe, turn left and walk
towards the pier.

Local fishermen use the beach and tie up their colourful boats in the lee of
this long arm stretching into the sea. Also on the leeward side is an area of
saltmarsh, colourful too in summer when the sea aster is in flower. The pier is
constructed from slag produced by the furnaces of the old ironworks. It is a joy
to walk but save your visit until your return.

Go under the iron bridge that links the shore with the pier and stroll the wonderful stretch of golden sand. Soon the houses of the village are left behind and
the foreshore is clothed with grass, reeds and masses of Isle of Man cabbage –
its common name is Dandy. Behind the pleasing vegetation towers a huge red
slag heap, now being softened by plants and a few saplings. Out on the sands,

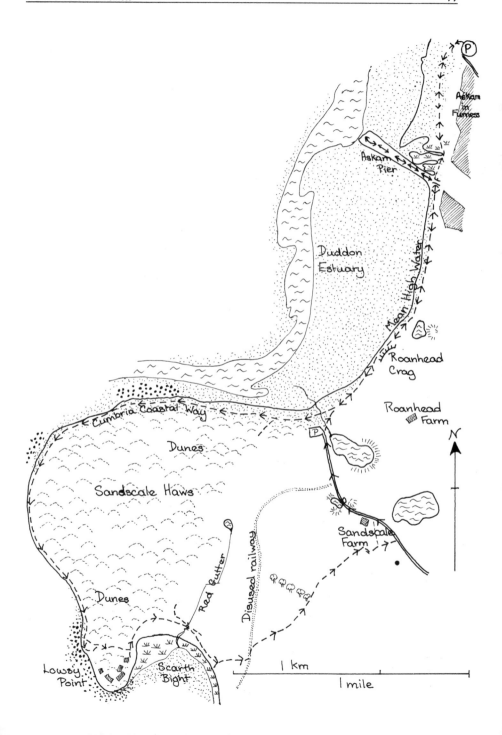

Askam in Furness

Askam Pier

Duddon Estuary

Mean High Water

Roanhead Crag

Roanhead Farm

N

Cumbria Coastal Way

Dunes

Sandscale Haws

Sandscale Farm

Red Gutter

Disused railway

Dunes

Lowsy Point

Scarth Bight

1 km

1 mile

fishermen dig for bait and others collect buckets of cockles from the sides of the criss-crossing channels.

Wind round the rocks of Roanhead Crag and go on. If you have binoculars, take some time to identify the huge numbers of birds feeding on the damp sand and

Ringed plovers and dunlin

bathing in the shallow rivulets. Ignore the sandy track coming down from Roanhead – this is your return route – and begin to walk seawards, with huge sand dunes now to your left. Notice the tough Marram grass, the roots of which bind the shifting sand.

As the dunes bear south, continue edging them. Look ahead to see the sea side of Walney Island, and then the enormous slag heap at Barrow comes into view. Continue on at the foot of the sand dunes, and as you come to a farm gate on your left, look for the pretty sea holly growing close by. Go through the gate and walk ahead on a wide grassy trod that brings you to several dwellings at Lowsy Point. Join a wide track, reinforced with small red grit, and bear left to wind round Scarth Bight, a vast area of salt marsh.

Cross Red Gutter, a narrow stream, on a tractor bridge and walk on to a 1939-45 war blockhouse. Beyond, where the track swings right, head left for a sturdy stile. The first few steps are along the bed of a dismantled railway and then the good track, waymarked, swings out into lush pastures.

As you near Sandscale farm, on your left, follow the waymark directing your right to join a narrow road. Turn left and walk, for half a mile, to where it ends, just above the shore (noted on your outward walk). Descend the sandy track and, if you have time, walk round the duckboarded pond, where you might view the rare Natterjack toads. Here an information board tells you about the toads and that the National Trust bought Sandscale Haws in 1984.

Go on towards the pier, rounding Roanhead Crag. Pass under the iron bridge and climb right a narrow path that takes you onto the pier. Stroll to the end. A few timbers remain where boats once tied up. In the cracks between the sheets of clinker about the pier end, look for clumps of sea campion thriving. As you return you might spot the dainty autumn gentian and seaside century colouring the sward that makes this pier such a delightful place.

Return to the path and continue to the steps to the parking area or to the station.

Walk 27: Dalton-in-Furness – Lindal-in-Furness

Dalton Castle – Tantabank Lane – above Standing Tarn – Cistercian Way – Little Urswick Crags – Lindal – beside Wild Animal Park – Dalton

Start/finish: Small parking area close to castle or parking bays along main street (GR 227739). Dalton has now been by-passed by the A590.

Type of walk: This 6½-miler starts from Dalton's castle and fine church. It continues over pastures where all traces of this once busy iron-ore mining area are now clothed in bushes or greensward. At Little Urswick Crags the path passes over hillocks where limestone outcrops most pleasingly. Then it's on to Lindal, which hides its charms from the busy A-road. Good grassy tracks and quiet roads for most of the way. One path is not easy to find on the ground, and the OS map is not helpful, but make full use of surrounding points of reference.

Map: OS Outdoor Leisure 6 (new series).

Public transport: Stagecoach Cumberland Barrow – Ulverston. Inquiries 01946 63222. North Western Trains. Inquiries 0345 484950.

Nearest towns: Barrow, Ulverston.

Refreshments and toilets: Dalton.

Dalton castle stands in the market place at the top of the now quiet refurbished main road. It stands close to the pleasant houses, which face the market place. Once Dalton was the largest town and had the most important market in Furness. The castle, a 14th century pele tower, was built by the monks of Furness Abbey to defend the people of Dalton and the approaches to the abbey. It had three upper floors, an entrance close to the south-east corner and a spiral stair-case in the west wall. By 1545 it was in a ruinous state and a year later, at the di-rection of Henry VIII, it was repaired at a cost of £20, using materials from Furness Abbey. It was a prison until 1774. Courts were held here until 1925. The castle now belongs to the National Trust and is open, free, from Easter to the end of September, on a Saturday, from 2pm to 5pm. Also in the market place is a splendid Victorian cast-iron drinking fountain. Behind the castle stands the church of St Mary, which looks into trees and fields. The building is one of the grandest by Paley and Austin, the church architects. George Romney, the painter, who was born in the town, is buried in the churchyard.

The Walk

With your back to the castle, walk down the road, past the drinking fountain, to take the next right turn, the road to Barrow. Cross with care and walk the few metres to cross the bridge over the often dry Poaka Beck. Immediately beyond, and before the next left turn off the main road, turn left into Little Fields, to walk a walled track, with the channel carrying the stream to your left.

Continue on this long track until you reach a road, where you turn right. Climb uphill past the pub, The Railway. Walkers arriving by train should join the

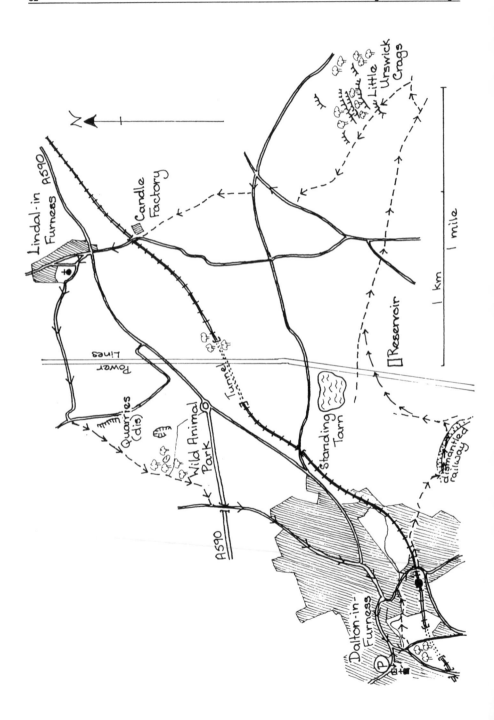

walk here. Cross the road bridge over the railway line and turn left into Tantamount Lane. Follow the road along and, continue as it climbs gently right, passing through much new housing. At the top of the slope, where the road bears sharp right, turn left to walk to a signposted kissing gate, into fields, between two houses.

Follow the hedge on the right to come to a waymarked stile over the fence. Beyond, head on across the pasture, towards the embankment of a disused mineral railway, to the top right corner. Go over the waymarked stile and on over the grassy embankment to a stile in the hedge ahead.

Beyond climb up the banking onto another grassy embankment. Turn left and stay on it until you reach the hedge (keep to the right of a trench used to dump rubbish). Drop left to the trench to climb the next stile. Walk on along the track (here the route of the path differs from the map) to pass to the right of a flooded open-cast pit, surrounded by grassy hillocks, once spoil tips from the mine. Hawthorn bushes and forest trees clothe the slopes, softening an area that must have once been noisy, muddy and extremely busy.

Drinking fountain, Dalton

Once beside the flooded pit, strike right, heading for two large pylons seen across the hummocky pasture. On a hill to your right is an enclosed reservoir. Well away to your left, and down a slope, is Standing Tarn, a pretty name for a disappointing pool.

Beyond the pylons continue on (no waymarks to help you and many sheep and cow trods to confuse), keeping below the sloping ground to reach the corner of a hedge. Go on in the same general direction to the next hedge. The rickety stile you take lies at an angle in the hedgerow, well to the left of a gate. Once over, the difficult part is completed and you have joined the Cistercian Way. Go ahead beside the hedge, on your left, to a signposted stile to a narrow road.

Cross and take a step to the right to look for the easy-to-miss stile set at the back of the thick hedge. Beyond, cross the pasture to the next stile, directly ahead (a very narrow gap stile) onto another minor road. Cross and go through yet another narrow stile. Pause here to enjoy a fine retrospective view of Black Combe.

Stroll up the pasture beside the wall on your right to pass through a waymarked gateless gap and on to take a gap stile into a pleasing hedged and grassy track. Continue down and down for 700 metres. Beyond a gate on the left, look for another hidden stile, in the hedge on the left. Head slightly right across the pasture to a gap stile in the wall. Beyond you enter a swelling sward of outcropping limestone. This is surely the place for your picnic.

Turn left and wind round, keeping parallel with the wall, to a gap stile beside a large gap. Continue ahead, with the clints and grykes of the limestone and ash and hawthorn trees mainly to your right. Once over the domed area, descend grassy slopes to a gate at the corner of two hedges. Pause here to look right to see the monument on Hoad Hill.

Beyond the gate walk ahead along another grassy hedged way until you join the narrow road once again. Turn right and descend gently to a crossroads, where you turn left. Fifty metres along, on the right, take an iron kissing gate into a pasture.

Walk down the pasture and over a little hillock, which obscures a sturdy stile until you are almost upon it. Beyond, climb the rough pasture to another kissing gate. Go on from here, beside the hedge on your right, to pass the Candle Works on your right. These were opened by Diana, Princess of Wales, in 1990.

Keep on to a gated stile to a narrow road. Turn right and cross the railway bridge. Go on ahead along the road, which is lined with three-storey cottages. These were built for railway workers and miners. Lindal station is now closed. At the end of the 19th century, as a result of extensive mining subsidence, an engine disappeared into a 70 metre hole that appeared in the railway sidings here. It was never seen again.

Walk on to take the light-controlled crossing over the A590. Walk ahead to the village green, a large grassy area surrounded by sycamore and horse chestnut trees and encircled by iron railings. This has been a green for only about a hundred years. Before that it was a tarn. Lindal is an ancient settlement and in 1220 it was recorded as a grange of Furness Abbey. St Peter's church stands to one side of the tree-fringed green and was built in 1885.

Leave the square, left, with the church to your right and follow the quiet road as it winds right, and then left, before continuing for 800 metres. Take the first left turn and, a few metres on, just beyond the access track to Tytup farm, climb the stile, on the right, signposted Hoghouse Brow. Walk straight ahead by the fence on your right, to the next stile. Continue ahead to go through a hedged, muddy way to another stile. Go on ahead, beside the fence on your left. To your right are more large hollows filled with water and surrounded with the familiar grassy mounds from earlier open-cast mining.

Go on by the hedge beyond which is the Wild Animal Park and from where come interesting calls. The clear path then decants you into the parking area for the Park. Walk left and then descend the access road, right. Turn left to cross the road bridge over the by-pass, to reach Hoghouse Brow.

Continue down the road and stay on it all the way to the main road at Dalton. Turn right to return to the parking area near the castle or, after a few metres, cross and walk along Station Road to the station.

Walk 28: Furness Abbey

Furness Abbey – Bow Bridge – Stank Lane – Stank Farm – Dendron – Harbarrow – Stainton with Adgarley – North Stank Farm – Newton – Furness Abbey

Start/finish: Use the museum car park (GR 217717) if you intend to visit Furness Abbey or the car park (GR 219715) half a mile nearer to Barrow-in-Furness. The abbey lies 1½ miles north of Barrow. To reach it leave Abbey Road – a wide, tree-lined road, one of the main access roads to Barrow's town centre – by one of two well signposted roads which lead off, east.

Type of walk: This pleasant 6-miler takes you over isolated rolling pastures east of Furness Abbey. The walk passes through several attractive villages and allows you to visit the wonderful Abbey and glorious Bow Bridge. There is some walking along quiet roads.

Map: OS Outdoor Leisure 6 (new series).

Public transport: Stagecoach Cumberland buses run along Abbey Road. Furness Abbey is less than ten minutes walk away. Inquiries 01946 63222. North Western trains to Barrow. Inquiries 0345 484950.

Nearest towns: Barrow, Dalton-in-Furness.

Refreshments: Snacks and meals at the Abbey Tavern.

Toilets: In car park.

The soaring red sandstone ruin of the abbey is often described as one of the best kept secrets of Furness. It is one of the most impressive architectural and historical monuments to be seen in Cumbria. The 700-year-old site once housed a flourishing community of a wealthy order, ranked only slightly lower than that of Yorkshire's Fountains Abbey. Its huge farming activities were largely responsible for the way parts of the Lake District look today. The abbey was and still is isolated, comparatively speaking, but the development of the harbour at Piel Island did much to improve access and trade. Piel Castle was built by the monks as a fortified warehouse for their grain and wool. It was also a smuggling den for them, enabling them to evade the high tariffs imposed by the King. But in 1537 the monastery and its possessions had to be given up to the King. Start your walk with a visit to the evocative ruins. Stroll round the site, enjoying a free audio-tour. For information on opening times etc, phone 01229 823420.

The Walk

From the free car park, walk right. Enjoy the grand vista of the abbey obtained from this spot. Just beyond a small, fine building on your right, the newly refurbished abbey mill, take the railed track into deciduous woodland. Look right to see the remains of the housing for the mill's waterwheel. The track brings you to the side of the railway line. Cross with extreme care and once through a white kissing gate, walk right to follow an indistinct path. This brings you to the side of Mill Beck, where you continue along the banking. Cross the

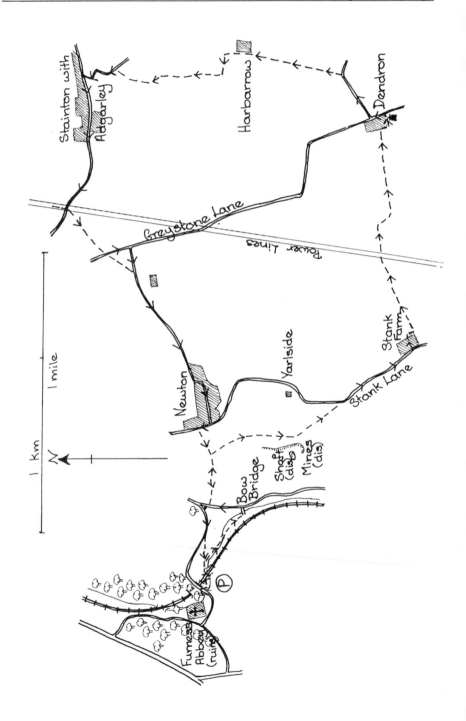

footbridge and stroll on along the clearer way to Bow Bridge, an ancient monument.

An information board suggests that the bridge dates from the 15th century. It crosses Mill Beck, carrying one of the medieval routes associated with Furness Abbey. It was intended for pedestrians and packhorses and it may have had stone parapets on either side.

Cross the bridge and continue to the road. Turn left to walk the tree-lined way to a small triangle of trees. Go through the kissing gate on the right, signposted Newton. Climb straight up the hill to the brow, walking a footpath of bright red soil. Do not pass through the kissing gate, but walk right, with the hedge to your left. As you go notice grassy hollows, bumps and fenced-off steep slopes, all part of the disused Yarlside iron mines.

As you near the brow, look for the easy-to-miss stile in the hedge on your left. Beyond stride diagonally across the large pasture, following the route of the telegraph lines, to a kissing gate onto Stank Lane. Turn right and continue on to pass between the stone abutments of a bridge that once carried the old tramway of the mines.

Go on to Stank Farm to turn left into the unsignposted yard (using the gate before the access track to the farmhouse), to pass between outbuildings. Bear left at the end of the barn on the left and then wind right, along the edge of a pasture, keeping beyond the fence above a large barn and then the farmhouse.

At the corner, ignore the gate, and turn left before the hedge and climb gently. Then descend the side of the vast undulating field to reach a waymarked stile. Beyond, and in a few steps, take the waymarked stile in the hedge on the left into another vast pasture.

Again climb gently with the hedge to your right and, once over the brow, begin to descend steadily, staying with the hedge, to pass below power lines. Climb the awkward stile (waymarked) in the bottom corner. Beyond, cross right to ascend once more. To your right, the hedge is formed by hawthorn bushes growing above a stone and turf wall.

Enjoy the pleasing rural view, at the brow, with the sands and waters of Morecambe Bay beyond. Then begin your descent towards Dendron farm and the church beside it. Go through the gate into the farmyard and wind right to the road. Turn right to visit the fine St Matthew's church, first built in 1642 and rebuilt in 1795. For nearly two centuries the school was held in the church and its famous pupil was the artist George Romney, who attended until he was 11. The church (he stipulated its use as a school) was paid for by a Robert Dickinson, who had been born in the nearby village of Leece.

Leave the church and walk left to re-pass Dendron farm. One of the cottages just beyond has a 1662 date-stone. Take the next right turn, a narrow hedged lane, to continue past a house to take a stile on the left, a signposted bridleway to Stainton. Head on from the stile, keeping beside the fence and hedge to the left.

Go past Harbarrow farm and continue where the track becomes metalled. Follow it where it turns left, and then right, and brings you to the edge of the village green at Stainton with Adgarley. The village is really two small ones with no boundary between them.

Turn left to walk towards the farm and then right to cross the small stream. Walk left across the green, where there are outcroppings of rock (the names of the two villages mean a place of rough stone). Across, on the far side, you can see the Farmers Arms and the Miners Arms, almost side by side, which show the village's past connection with farming and iron ore mining.

Look behind the goal post furthest away from the pubs to see the faint outline of an old cockfighting ring. Continue diagonally across the grass to the road, which you cross, and walk on for a few yards. Pause here to look across at Stainton Hall (1638), a manor house with mullioned windows and a huge square chimney stack. Part of it is believed to have been demolished by cannon fire during the Civil War.

From now on use the pavement and then the grass verge as you leave the village. Stand in the entrance to a grassy lane on the right, under the overhead power lines, to locate the stile on the opposite side of the road. This is the way the walk continues. At the time of writing the signpost lies on the ground.

Go through the gap stile and take another, opposite. Walk diagonally uphill, to pass through a gap in the hedge and then continue to take an awkward stile to Greystone Lane. Turn left and walk the quiet way. Take the next right and walk on past North Stank farm. Continue on the narrow road as it descends gently into Newton, a village once surrounded by mining activity. Go past a tiny green with three horse chestnut trees and then the Farmers Arms pub. Go past the war memorial standing in a neat fenced green.

Follow the road as it winds right, where you can see several rows of workers' cottages, to come to the fine three-storied Village Inn. Opposite to it is a kissing gate. Pass through and continue to another directly ahead (the one you ignored on your outward route). Descend the "red" footpath to take the kissing gate to the triangle of trees. Walk ahead in the direction of the abbey and, a short distance along the road, use the footpath on the left to regain the white kissing gate, passed through when crossing the railway line. Retrace your outward route to the abbey.

Bow Bridge

Walk 29: Walney Island – North End

Earnse Point, Walney Island – North End Haws – North End Rabbit Warren – Earnse Point

Start/finish: Earnse Bay car park (GR 171699). To reach the island, leave Barrow-in-Furness by the Jubilee Bridge. Once over, turn right and follow the road until just beyond the Periscope pub (on the left), where you turn right again. Continue ahead to the shoreline and the car park lies to the left.

Type of walk: An excellent 6-miler through sand dunes and by dune slacks. Part of the walk is along the shoreline. Though the terrain is mainly level, sturdy shoes or boots make for easier walking over the sand and the rabbit-hole pocked turf. There are no waymarks and no restrictions. As you walk to the point, keep the channel and the mainland to your right and, on your return, keep the sea to your right. During the summer months it is a naturalist's paradise, with its plethora of wild flowers, and this walk gives some idea of what can be seen in August.

Map: OS Outdoor Leisure 6 (new series).

Nearest town: Barrow-in-Furness.

Public transport: Stagecoach Cumberland bus 1/1A serves South Walney. Inquiries 01946 63222.

Refreshments: Walney and Barrow.

Toilets: In car park.

Walney Island is linked to mainland Barrow-in-Furness by the very fine Jubilee Bridge. Vickerstown, Walney's main residential area, was built to house the burgeoning workforce employed in Barrow. But Walney's first residents could have been a Stone Age family. In the 1950s archaeologists discovered a site where flint axe heads were honed and fine-finished. They believe that the axe heads were made in Langdale and then, when the weather and the food supply deteriorated, the family worked and wintered on Walney. There were plenty of oysters, cockles and razorshells to live on and the occasional deer that swam across to feed on the island.

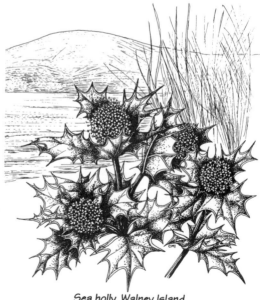

Sea holly, Walney Island

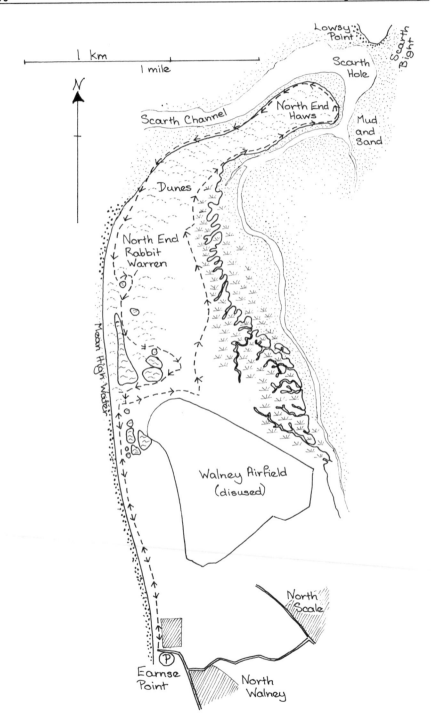

The Walk

From the car park, walk the rough road to pass in front of a row of holiday homes, with the sea to your left. Carry on along the road to its end and then go on the continuing grassy path. As you go, look for sea holly, sea spurge, sea cabbage and the lovely mountain pansy.

Follow the narrow path as it swings right (inland) to come beside a fence on your right to pass through low sand dunes. Go on along one of several grassy paths and tracks to pass several ponds on your left. These were formed when gravel was removed. Today a family of swans and many mallards swim serenely beyond the broad fringe of bulrush and lesser bulrush.

Go on along the pleasing way, where yarrow and sneezewort yarrow thrive, to an information board and the start of the nature reserve. Close by you might be able to spot some trenches. These were used in the 1914-18 war to train young soldiers before they set off for France.

As you walk, look for tall parasol mushrooms sticking up above the vegetation. As they ripen the top opens to form the familiar umbrella shape. The identification books say that this is one of the best of the edible species.

And then the way continues through a vast stretch of sweet smelling heather, where bell heather and cross-leaved heath thrive in the now more acid soil. As you continue on the pleasing path look for a vast sward of sea lavender and sea aster stretching away towards the channel to your right.

Continue on, walking to the right of fencing put there to keep sheep off the shore. If there is an exceptionally high tide, use the stiles to gain access to the other side of the fence. The sheep have been introduced to keep the grass shorter, encouraging the rarer plants found on the reserve to thrive.

Go through a kissing gate and stroll on towards the north end of the island, with enormous sand dunes to the left. This is the area, in which archaeologists believe a Stone Age family lived. Continue to the point.

Look across Scarth Channel to see the settlement at Lowsy Point, passed through in walk 26. Once round the point take a narrow path, on the west side of the island, which runs through the very shallow dunes. Step with care, because many rabbit holes lie below the marram grass. These rabbits are believed to have descended from those brought to the island in medieval times by the monks of Furness Abbey to be bred and raised for food.

As you near the very high dunes, passed on the other side, on your way to the point, step down onto the shore and go on. At low tide you can see the wreck of a ship and cormorants standing on it, with wings outstretched, helping to digest their fish diet.

Continue on for half a mile and then move into the shallow dunes on a good path. Very soon there is a maze of narrow paths. Take one that heads in a southerly direction. Look for tiny shallow pools surrounded by bramble and willow. Here the rare natterjack toad breeds.

Follow the path back to the fence, passed at the outset of your walk, and continue beside it to reach the shore again. Turn left, with the sea to your right, to return to the car park.

Walk 30: Walney Island – South End

Nature reserve car park – Bank Hide – Observation Hide – Pier Hide – Bay Hide – Groyne Hide – Sea Hide – Fort – Heligoland Trap – Gate Pool – Car park

Start/finish: Reserve car park (GR 215622). The reserve is situated at the southern tip of Walney Island, six miles south of Barrow-in-Furness. Follow the A590 to Barrow and cross Jubilee Bridge onto Walney island. Turn left immediately and follow Ocean Road for 3/4 mile. Turn left into Carr Lane and continue for four miles, passing Biggar Village. An unmetalled road, bearing right, near the entrance to the South End caravan site, leads to the reserve car park after one mile.

Type of walk: A delightful 3½ – 4-miler on a well waymarked trail that takes you all round the reserve. You are asked to keep strictly to the trail and to watch your step, as some birds may nest on the paths. Head protection is advisable between May and July as a precaution against aggressive gulls. The hides are well placed for viewing various habitats. The paths are sandy and the tracks are reinforced. A pleasing walk for all and an ornithologist's dream.

Map: OS Outdoor Leisure 6 (new series) or obtain a trail guide at the car park kiosk. Here you also buy your permit, which includes parking (£1.80 as this book went to press).

Toilets: Car park.

NB: The reserve is closed on Mondays, except bank holidays. Opening times are 10am – 5pm (4pm winter). No dogs are allowed between April and August and they must be kept on a lead at all other times.

South Walney Nature Reserve is run by the Wild Life Trust, Cumbria. It is noted for its massive population of breeding gulls and eider duck. Its range of habitats includes sand dunes, mudflats, salt marsh, freshwater marsh and brackish pools.

Walney Island was formed at the end of the ice age when retreating glaciers left deposits of clay, rock and sand. Archaeological evidence suggests that the island was inhabited by man shortly after its formation. Early inhabitants probably included birds among their food.

Piel Castle stands on Piel Island, south of Barrow, and is reached by a ferry from Roa Island. It was built in 1327. The substantial remains are ruinous but they make a dramatic sight, viewed from South Walney. In 1487, Lambert Simnel, a merchant's son, landed at Piel. He claimed that he was the rightful King of England. With an army of German and Irish mercenaries, he set off across Furness to march on London. He was defeated by King Henry VII at the battle of Stoke.

The Walk

From the car park go past the toilets and the coastguard cottages (wardens' homes) and walk on the grassy reinforced fenced way to visit bank hide. This

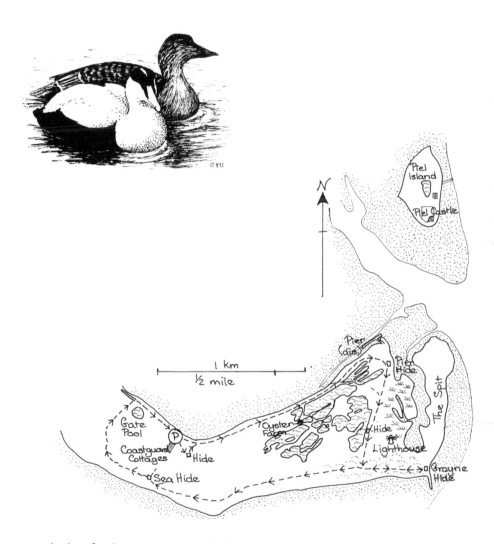

overlooks a freshwater scrape and is the haunt of a variety of waders, including sandpiper and ruff.

Return to the car park and enjoy, ahead, the grand view of Piel Castle across Walney Channel. Leave by the gate at the back of the parking area to follow the bright red marker posts across a pasture to the flagstaff and to enter the observation hide. From here you can view the gull colony during the breeding season. A wall display from Niko Tinbergen's book "Signals for Survival" tells the story of gull behaviour.

From the hide, walk in the direction of the castle to join the waymarked rein-forced track and stroll on, with the castle, over the channel, to your left. In sum-mer look to the shingle strand on your left to see horned poppy, sea campion and black nightshade. Go on to pass the oyster farm to your right and also sev-eral freshwater and saline pools, the latter the result of gravel extraction. Here you might see redshank and greenshank, teals, mergansers and goldeneye, at the right time of the year.

Continue on towards the remnants of the old pier, the track, in summer, lined with a mass of the exotic blue-purple viper's bugloss. Then follow the red posts, right, to visit pier hide overlooking Lighthouse Bay and the Spit (there is no access to the Spit). From here, in autumn, winter and spring, you can see the roosting area of thousands of waders. As you walk on along the track look out for a mass of mauve and yellow dune pansies, flowering between harsh leaves of marram grass.

Visit the bay hide next, observing the request asking you not to proceed along the private track to the lighthouse. Here marram grass, holding the sand, dominates the vegetation. The hide overlooks pools.

Go on the waymarked trail through very shallow dunes. Turn left and walk a narrow path, with the sea to your right, to visit groyne hide, which overlooks Morecambe Bay. Look for various species of terns, divers, auks and grey seals. At various times of the year you might also spot eiders, turnstones and grey plo-vers. Enjoy the huge stretch of sand, which looks like an inland desert when the tide is out and like an inland sea when it is full.

Return back along the narrow path through the shallow dunes and then con-tinue on along the foreshore, where the huge breakers of the Irish Sea pound the pebble beach on wild and stormy days. In early autumn the grassy way is bright red with flowering orache. On either side of the path grow sea rocket, sea beet and the tall and striking henbane. This area is known as gull meadow and is a place where, during the breeding season, you need to wear a hat.

Then the red posts direct you away from the shore, through South End rab-bit warren, to bring you to the sea hide, overlooking the Irish Sea. This is a great spot from which to watch sea birds, but you may need a telescope to see those that fly far out over the waves.

Continue on along the foreshore until you near a war-time look-out post. The trail then leads you inland, to pass a wood-and-net construction known as a heligoland trap. Here staff ring migrating birds as part of a nation-wide study into the migration and distribution of various species.

Join the main track to the reserve to walk right, passing gate pool on the right, where you might spot more waders and duck. Continue on to return to the parking area.

Walk 31: Rampside – Leece

*Rampside – St Michael's church – Page Bank farm – Moss Side farm –
Moss House – Leece – Bracken Bed Lane – Coast Road – Rampside*

Start/finish: Roadside parking close to the telephone box at Rampside (GR
239662), which is situated 5 miles from Barrow-in-Furness and nine miles from
Ulverston. A narrow road leaves the A5087 at the roundabout, where the A-road
makes a right-angled turn.

Type of walk: A good 6-miler through quiet rolling pastures to a pretty village, its
houses clustered around a tarn, with ducks and geese. Much of the walk is well
waymarked but when the vegetation is lush these marks can be difficult to spot. Paths
and farm tracks might be muddy after rain. The return is along the Coast Road (Cumbria Coastal Way), with fine views of Piel, Walney and Roa Islands. Use the footpath
beside the road or walk along the sands for much of the way.

Map: OS Outdoor Leisure 6 (new series).

Public transport: Stagecoach Cumberland 11/12 Barrow – Ulverston. Inquiries
01946 63222

Nearest towns: Barrow, Ulverston.

Refreshments: Rampside.

---

*In 1840 St Michael's Church, Rampside, was built as a replacement for an ear-
lier chapel built in 1621, which in turn stood on the site of a Saxon burial barrow.
It stands more than half a mile outside the village. In 1652 George Fox, the
Quaker, visited the earlier church. Rampside, a seaside village much in favour
with the Victorians, straggles along the shore at the eastern entrance to Piel Harbour. The name means "ram's head" because the land on which it stands is sup-
posed to look like such a head. Leece, mentioned in the Doomsday Book, means
"an open space in woodland". Its pleasing cottages and houses border a triangle
of roads around a delightful tarn.*

The Walk

Take the footpath opposite the telephone box, signposted "Westfield Point".
Continue on the good track, with houses to your left and, to your right, a hedge
which in autumn is heavily laden with hips, haws, elderberries, blackberries and
honeysuckle berries.

After just over half a mile, ignore the stile on the right and go on for another
half mile to take the waymarked gate on the right. Head across a short pasture,
with a fence to the left, to climb a stile. Go on, with the fence to your right, to
pass through a sturdy kissing gate. Stroll on, ignoring the stile on the right, and
continue to pass through a gate in the fence, just before the busy A-road. Walk a
rising grassy trod to a stile onto the road, beside the striking church of St Michael's, which is a good guide in navigating your way across the pastures.

The church is generally locked but you may wish to walk round the outside.
Look for the plaque at the foot of the tower, which gives you the name of the

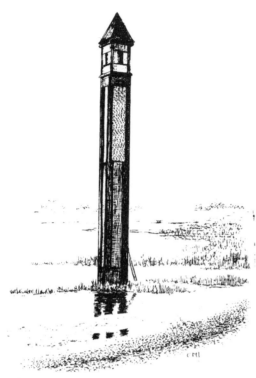

Lighthouse, Rampside

joiner and those of the wallers who helped in its construction. Cross the main road, with care, and continue down Peasholme Road, a narrow hedged lane. At the T-junction turn right and then, almost immediately, go left down an even narrower lane with grass growing down the middle. Notice the bright green ferns below the ash trees of the hedge.

Follow the metalled way as it swings left to pass between two dwellings, labelled Newtown on the map. Stroll 50 metres on the continuing hedged track and, where it swings left; look for an easy-to-miss stile on the right. Beyond, cross left to the side of a small stream, which you go over on a well waymarked stiled footbridge. As the stiles and bridge are below the banking of the stream they are difficult to spot.

Walk ahead, with the hedge to your left and then, where the hedge moves away, keep right of the small hillock ahead to come to a gate into the outbuildings of Moss Side farm. Walk ahead to pass between the barns and well to the right of the farmhouse and continue on a reinforced way to a gate. Head diagonally right to a footbridge over Sarah Beck. Continue on ahead and then gently ascend a grassy track, keeping to the left side of Moss House.

Climb the stile beside an ornate gate and go on along the access track, which brings you to the edge of the tarn in the centre of Leece. Walk anti-clockwise around the pond to a seat where you might wish to pause. Walk on a little further beside the water and then look right to see the footpath that takes you on your return route. The waymark is on telegraph pole, numbered 23 50 06, and is easy to miss. Climb the narrow hedged path between houses. Once through the narrow stile, walk with the hedge on your right and stay by the hedge to a stile in the corner of two hedges (a tricky gap stile where you will have to lift your feet high).

Stride on ahead, steadily descending, to a gate in the corner. Beyond, turn right to walk Bracken Bed Lane, a wide pleasing hedged track. Cross a narrow

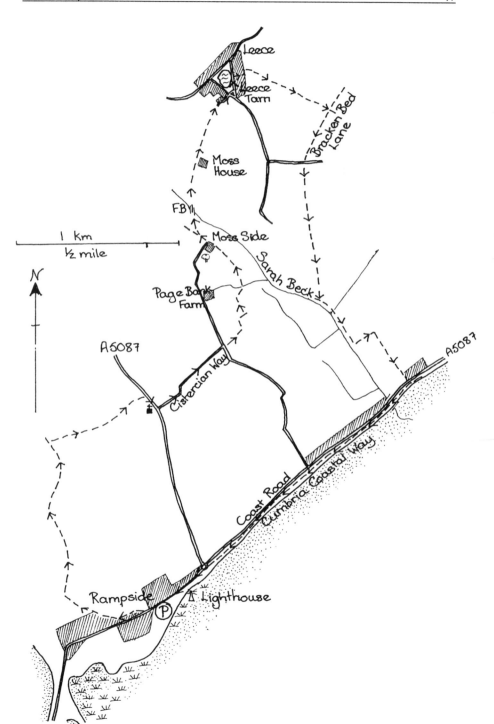

road and go on. Where the hedged way ceases walk on beside the hedge to your right. Continue to the corner, where you cross a stream by a footbridge. Go on to climb two more stiles and then bear left, across a pasture, to a gate onto a lane. Turn right and walk the well kept way and then the continuing Meadow Lane to the Coast Road.

Cross and walk right. Here you can remain on the footpath along the embanked way or go down on the shore and continue. As you near the roundabout, shore walkers should rejoin the road and then turn left off the main road to walk into Rampside.

As you go look for the tall square-shaped unmanned lighthouse on the shore, a navigational light-tower for vessels entering the Walney Channel.

Almost opposite is Rampside Hall, a late 17th century house. On the roof is a row of 12 diagonally set chimneys, known as the Twelve Apostles. Legend relates that a young man wished to marry but the father of the would-be bride said his daughter could marry only a man rich enough to have a house with a dozen chimneys. So the young man built the hall with 12 chimneys all in a line, and at each wedding anniversary smoke issued from all of them. Walk on to your parking area.

You may wish to extend your walk to pass the Concle Inn, built on a gravel pit filled with saline water and used for recuperative swims. From here you might like to stroll the causeway to Roa Island, a stimulating climax to your walk on a breezy day.

From Roa you can sometimes go by ferry to Piel Island. There are also guided walks across the treacherous sands to the island.

Walk 32: Gleaston

Gleaston Mill – Gleaston Castle – Scales – Scales Park – Aldingham –
Newbiggin – Deep Meadow Beck – Gleaston

Start/finish: At Gleaston Mill (GR 261708), where the owners are quite happy for you to use their car park unless it is full. Please go to the mill and say that you wish to leave your car. (See suggestions for alternative parking half-way along the walk.)

Type of walk: This quiet 6½-mile walk through Low Furness starts at a working mill, continues to a sadly ruinous castle and goes on to the village of Scales. It then takes you through lush pastures to the edge of Morecambe Bay. After visiting a historic church, it returns through the pleasant villages of Newbiggin and Gleaston. It is generally level walking. The tracks near farms can be very muddy after heavy rain. The stiles, gates and waymarkings are good.

Map: OS Outdoor Leisure 6 (new series).

Nearest towns: Barrow-in-Furness, Ulverston.

Public transport: Stagecoach Cumberland from Barrow or Ulverston, inquiries 01946 63222

Refreshments/toilets: Gleaston Mill.

Gleaston mill dates from 1774. It ground grain for farmers from Low Furness, its 5.5 metre diameter wheel turning four huge stones to produce oat and wheat flour. It fell into disrepair in 1948 but in 1990, after loving restoration by the present owners, the mighty wheel, with its 36 larch wood buckets, began turning again.

Gleaston Castle

The Walk

Walk north, right, out of the car park, along the walled and hedged lane to pass a sturdy old lime kiln and continue to Cowsill Farm (1850).

Beyond stand the ruins of Gleaston Castle, believed to have been built in the 14th century for defence against marauding Scots. It was constructed in great haste, and clay-infill (still to be seen) was used instead of mortar. It was lived in for barely a century and soon became a ruin – the lack of mortar probably hastening this process.

The ivy-clad castle is now the property of the National Trust, which intends to do work on it when it has funds. To visit the ruins ask at the farmhouse – the castle stands on the farm's land. The farmer's bull and cows sometimes graze the pasture beneath the ruined abutments.

Go on along the lane to pass the reed-fringed Mere Tarn on the right. Head on to take the second footpath on the left. Beyond the gap stile, stride across the pasture to the hedge, turn right and continue to join a track. Bear right to walk into the village of Scales.

Turn right again to saunter the single street, which is lined with houses of all sizes, dates and shapes. Pass Aldingham parish hall, once a malt kiln. Continue past the disused school, believed to have been a tithe barn earlier, and the attractive play area. Stride on past a neat triangle of grass, on your left, and follow the signpost for Aldingham.

Continue for a few yards along the road. Take the footpath on your right, also signposted Aldingham (the post at the time of writing is almost hidden by vegetation), to walk a grassy, walled track to a gate.

Beyond, walk diagonally right across the corner of the pasture to a double stile in the hedgerow. Turn left and pass through a gate to continue by the hedge on your left. Look for the stile in the middle of the lower hedge. Once over, descend the fine limestone steps and walk ahead to another waymarked stile.

Go on to follow the track as it swings above the outbuildings of Scales Park farm. Beyond the next gate, turn right and continue on the track to pass in front of the farmhouse (1840). Go through the next three gates. Where the track swings right and into the middle of the pasture, leave it left to pass through a gate. Walk beside the short fence on the right and turn right at the hedge to go through a waymarked gate.

From here, the clear stiled way goes on, with a hedge to your left and a good view of the Bay ahead. Here, in the rolling pastures, oyster catchers feed among the sheep. Stroll on to take a gap stile to the Coast Road (A5087), which you cross.

Turn left and take the right branch to pass Ladycroft Cottage. Stride on to visit the 12th century church of St Cuthbert, Aldingham. Go inside the spacious building, which has many Norman features. Look for the squint, or hagioscope, which enabled worshippers to see the celebration of the Sacrament. Another hole, probably for lepers, is set in the wall to the right of the altar. The bread would have been passed to the lepers on a long-handled shovel of wood.

Then sit on one of the seats in the churchyard, perhaps for your picnic, and

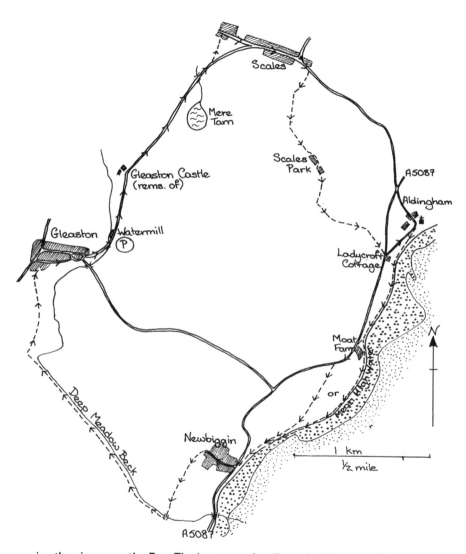

enjoy the view over the Bay. The buttressed wall was built by John Stonard, rector from 1814 to 1849 – erratic rocks from the seashore were used. He was also responsible for the construction of the very fine Aldingham Hall, just across the road from the church. (Between the church and toilets there is a large lay-by where you could park if the mill is full – then start the walk from this point.)

To continue the walk, return (south), in the direction from which you have come, but this time use the Cumbria Coastal Way along the shore if the tide is suitable. (If not, walk back along the Coast Road.)

Stride the mixture of sand, cobbles and pebbles. From here, if the day is clear, you should see Blackpool Tower. Pass Ladycroft Cottage, now on the right. Stroll on below low clay cliffs and then higher ones, and some that are terraced as part of erosion control.

Go on to pass Moat farm, tucked away among trees, and continue under very high cliffs. (If, once again, the tide is high, walk inland, past the farm and take the signposted way, going off left, along the top of the cliffs.) Stride on, with Piel Island coming into view. Pass a three-armed signpost, where both routes unite. Go by several dwellings and stay on the shore, using a wide rough track to come to the side of the Coast Road. Continue along the verge for 50 metres and then cross to take the right turn to walk into the tiny hamlet of Newbiggin.

Stroll ahead and go on to pass the farmhouse. Beyond, walk the continuing farm track. Where it divides, ignore the right turn and press on along the hedged and reinforced way. Go through the narrow stile to the left of the gate. Then take the waymarked gate on the right and walk left between the small sewage plant and the hedge. If the way is too overgrown, you may have to walk all round the outside of the sewage site – or ignore the waymarked gate and, beyond, take the stile in the right-hand corner of the field.

Cross the footbridge over the Deep Meadows Beck and turn right. Walk for just a mile along the arrowed and stiled way beside the stream. When the author last went this way, the fields had cereal crops growing right up to the path. The path itself, on the edge of the stream bank, was deep in seeding grasses and care was required in places to proceed along the narrow rough way. If, when you pass, the young frisky bullocks are in the pasture by the stream, use the path beyond the wire fence.

Ignore the gate to the right and pass through a metal gate ahead onto a wide, hedged track. Turn right and walk into the village of Gleaston. At the T-junction go right and continue. At the crossroads, follow the waterwheel road sign to return to the mill.

Walk 33: Great Urswick

Great Urswick – Little Urswick Crags – Little Urswick – Sunbrick – Stone Circle – Birkrigg Common – Birkrigg – Urswick Tarn – Great Urswick

Start/finish: The front of the Sunday school, next to the parish church of St Mary and St Michael, Great Urswick (GR 268742). Please park tidily. If there is a wedding or a funeral, all the space will be taken and you will have to find somewhere else.

Type of walk: A delightfully easy 6-miler. It starts from the village of Urswick, which lies in a fertile valley at the foot of a ridge of limestone. Through the vale flows Tarn Beck, which issues from Urswick Tarn. This reed-fringed lake is the haunt of coot and often visited by heron and geese. It is a walk of many stiles, some very narrow, many a delight to climb, from the top of which there are some pleasing views.

Map: OS Outdoor Leisure 6 (new series).

Nearest towns: Dalton-in-Furness, Ulverston.

Public transport: Stagecoach Cumberland, Barrow-Urswick-Ulverston, inquiries 01946 63222.

Refreshments: Great Urswick.

Walk towards the village, right (north), with pleasing glimpses of the tarn to your right. Just beyond the General Burgoyne public house, turn left into a narrow lane, which almost immediately ceases to be metalled.

Walk the hedged track and then take the right of two gates. Follow the grassy way, with outcrops of limestone and ash trees scattered over the pasture, and continue, with the wall to your left, to a stile. Beyond, stroll on and then take the next gate on your left. Once through, walk a little to the right and then left above more scattered trees about more limestone. As you go, notice the rocks to your right, marked as an ancient burial chamber on the OS map.

Drop down to the stile ahead and, once over, cross the pasture to a sign-posted gate to a narrow road. Cross to take the stile opposite and then another a few yards ahead. Climb straight uphill to a waymarked ladder stile, on the right, into woodland. The next stile gives access to more pasture. Away to your left and a short distance from the right of way are two Iron Age enclosures, one oval in plan and the other rectangular. The latter contains five hut circles.

Go ahead with the wood to your right, heading for a gap stile that has one stone faintly painted white. Beyond, turn left to walk a pleasant hedged path. Where it swings sharply right, pass through a gap stile on the left. Bear slightly left to climb over Little Urswick Crags, with woodland to your far left. Saunter on to a gap stile and then over pasture to climb a magnificent limestone stile.

Bear slightly left across more outcrops to a ladder stile and then continue along the waymarked way to Little Urswick. Cross the road to take the sign-posted way, straight ahead through farm buildings and two kissing gates, to Braithwaite Lane. Turn right and, after 75 metres, go through a very narrow squeeze stile on the left. Climb uphill beside the hedge on the right to a kissing

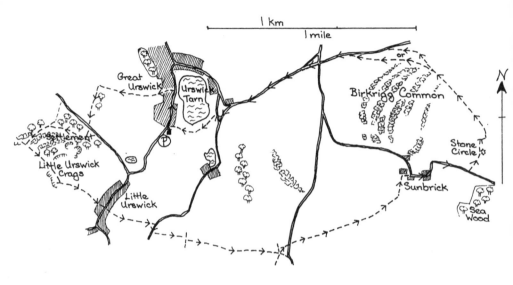

gate in the top right corner. Beyond, turn right and, after 10 metres, pass through another squeeze stile on your left.

Stride ahead across the next two stiled pastures. To the left, again off the right of way, are the remains of an Iron Age or Romano-British settlement, marked as an enclosure on the map. Just before the stile ahead in the wall, bear slightly left to walk to the road, which you cross to a hedged track.

Stride the glorious way, with increasing views of Morecambe Bay as you climb the low ridge, then descend to the little settlement of Sunbrick. At the road, turn left to walk uphill to see, on the left, a walled enclosure, once the site of Quaker burials. Then return downhill, passing Higher and then Lower Sunbrick. Both the latter and Sunbrick Cottage have 17th century date-stones. Continue on the road almost to the start of woodland on your right. Then take a grassy ride on your left, through the bracken on Birkrigg Common, for 200 metres to see the small stone circle. This was probably a cremation circle and would have contained burial urns. The view from here is magnificent.

Walk north, keeping parallel with the wall on your right. Ignore the gate and go on following the wall, still on your right, to the brow of the common, where another grand view awaits, this time of the Lakeland mountains. At the wall corner follow one of several grassy swathes, bearing steadily left through the bracken, and descend to White Gill Lane.

Continue ahead along the grassy verge, with the road to your right, until you reach a crossroads. Cross and, still continuing ahead, go downhill in the direction of Urswick. Take the first left and, at the bottom of a short hill, go sharp right along a narrow lane.

A signposted footpath on the left takes you around the south end of the tarn,

Stone circle, Birkrigg Common

over an obvious footbridge. Continue to a gate into the churchyard. In the porch look for the deep grooves made by Tudor soldiers sharpening their arrows. On the left side of the door is a well worn "sundial" of scratches which, using shadows, showed the time for masses and services.

It you still have time, visit the church, which is believed to date from the middle of the tenth century, if not before. It has undressed stone walls and a beamed ceiling. Look for the three-tiered Georgian pulpit and an altar painting of the Last Supper by James Cranke, a local painter, born in 1707. A small guidebook available in the church describes its many interesting contents. They include carved woodwork, ancient brasses and a 13th century hagioscope – a squint hole for those worshippers not allowed into the chancel to see the celebration of the Mass.

Walk 34: Ulverston – Pennington

The Gill – Rosside farm – High Greaves farm – Channel House – Copse Hill Plantation – Fellside farm – Fellside House – Rosside – The Gill

Start/finish: The Gill short stay (3 hours) pay and display car park, Ulverston (GR 285785).

Type of walk: This 4½-miler takes you through quiet countryside on footpaths that link several farms. A variety of land is traversed: pasture and fields, scattered copses and moorland. After rain the farm tracks can be very muddy and good footwear is essential. It is easy to combine this walk with the next one (35) when you should choose a long stay car park in Ulverston – all well signposted.

Map: OS Outdoor Leisure 6 (new series).

Nearest town: Ulverston.

Public transport: Stagecoach Cumberland buses from Barrow or Kendal, inquiries 01946 63222. Short walk to The Gill from Ulverston Station, North Western Trains, inquiries 0345 484950.

Refreshments: Cafes, restaurants, and pubs in Ulverston.

Toilets: Close to The Gill car park.

The earliest record of Pennington was in the Doomsday survey of 1086.

The Walk

Leave The Gill car park by the west end to walk a wide track signposted "Public footpath Gill Banks and the start of the Cumbria Way". Where it branches, take the left fork and continue to a stone bridge on your left. Cross and climb the delightful walled way to pass through a sturdy kissing gate onto a quiet road.

Turn left and after 50 metres take a kissing gate on the right, just before the entrance to a large house. Go ahead, with new houses over the wall to your left, to walk a long pasture to a kissing gate in the corner. Beyond take another gate on the left, a short distance along the hedge. Go on with the hedge to the right. Stroll through more kissing gates to come to Rosside farm and a narrow lane.

Turn right and, almost immediately, go through a gate on your left or use the stile beside it. Walk on with the hedge to your right and stay with it until you reach a very narrow lane. Here turn left and stroll the leafy way to continue over a crossroads. Go on past, on your left, High Greaves House, to take a gate on the right, signposted Channel House.

Climb steadily to join a cart track in the top right corner. Beyond the gate, turn left to walk towards Channel House farm. Cross a small stream, go through two gates and turn left towards the attractive farmhouse. Walk right, in front of it and, where the track swings left, turn right to stride a track that runs beside a wall of Pennington House.

Alder catkins

Go through the gate at the end of the track. Walk straight uphill to a gate in the top right corner. Go on over a tiny stream and continue climbing gently, with oak and alder to your right, to a signpost beyond a gate at a bend in a road. Ignore the road and turn sharp right to ascend a wide track, with Copse Hill Plantation to your right.

Once beyond the trees, enjoy the glorious view from this high-level way. You can see a large stretch of the Levens estuary, with Chapel Island seeming to float like a leaf. You also have a good view of Hoad monument. Pass through a gate and step out along the continuing way over the moorland pastures. At its end, climb the stile on the right to descend steadily along another pleasing track, with more extensive views ahead.

Watch out for the waymarked gate on your left, at the point where the track swings right. Beyond the gate, follow the wall and then cross the pasture, dropping downhill towards Fellside farm. Go through the waymarked gate at the back of the farmhouse (it can be very wet here) and turn left.

Walk ahead and, where the track winds right, take the easy-to-miss gate on the left. Walk ahead over a pasture to a small gate into the copse of Fellside House. (The walk from the track to this small gate can also be exceedingly wet – pick your way very carefully.)

Keep to the left of a barn and a greenhouse, and go ahead to another gate (all waymarked). Continue ahead, keeping in the same general direction, to another gate. Beyond walk on, still on the same contour, to pass a wooden bungalow and then press on to join a narrow road. Turn right to walk into the hamlet of Rosside. Wind left past the post-box and the telephone box. Stroll on for nearly half a mile to pass Tarn Close and to reach a T-junction.

Here walk right. Just beyond a seat on the left, take the walled track on the left, the way climbed almost at the outset of your walk. Cross the stone bridge. To return to The Gill, turn right.

To combine this ramble with walk 35, cross the bridge and turn left.

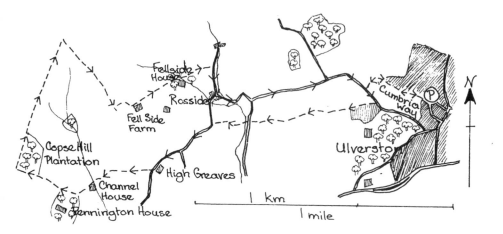

Walk 35: Ulverston – Hoad Hill and Monument

The Gill, Ulverston – Gill Banks – Old Hall Road – Flan Hill – Chittery Lane, Town Bank – Hoad Hill and monument – Ulverston

Start/finish: The Gill short stay (3 hours) pay and display car park, Ulverston (GR 285785). See walk 34.

Type of walk: This 3½-miler takes you out of the small town on a pleasing track, then on through woodland followed by quiet pastures below Flan Hill. After some unavoidable road walking, the way goes along a narrow leafy lane, leading to a good track, which takes you to the monument on Hoad Hill. Still the delight continues with a zig-zag down the bracken-clad slopes and a return to the car park along wide alleyways and narrow roads.

Map: OS Outdoor Leisure 6 (new series).

Nearest town: Ulverston.

Public transport: See walk 34.

Refreshments and toilets: See walk 34.

The Hoad Monument

The 30-metre monument on Hoad Hill is an imitation of the Eddystone Lighthouse. It was erected in 1850 to commemorate Sir John Barrow, the geographer and under-secretary to the Admiralty. He was born in a cottage in Ulverston.

The Walk

Walk west out of the end of The Gill along the wide tarmacked track, signposted "Public footpath, Gill Banks. Start of the Cumbria Way". Continue on, keeping to the left fork where the way divides. Ignore the footbridge over the beck and climb steadily through the trees. Then follow where the good track descends, before leaving the trees by a sturdy kissing gate.

Go on, enjoying the lovely valley ahead, to a similar gate to Old Hall Road. Cross and take the gate into the pastures below Flan Hill, where you are asked to remain on the foot-

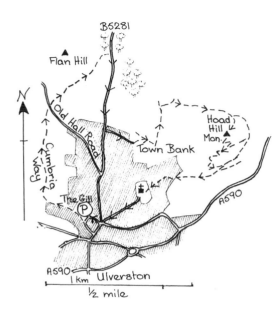

path. The clear way, with more kissing gates, remains beside the wall on the right.

A final gate gives access to the B5281, where you turn right. Walk, with care, for 500 metres to take the first left turn, Chittery Lane. After a short steepish climb it bears right and soon becomes a delightful, narrow hedged way. Continue where it winds right and go on along the narrowing way until you reach an open area, with seats about higher ground to your left. Ahead is a fine view of the monument on Hoad Hill (433ft/132m).

Bear left up the open ground, keeping beside the wall on the right. Go through a gate into a pleasing walled narrow track to reach another gate. Pass through and walk ahead to join a wider track and follow it right. The track has been reinforced in places and there are seats along the way from where you can look down on Ulverston and the Leven Estuary. Stroll on and keep with the track as it winds right, gently ascending to the foot of the monument. If the ground-level flag is flying, the monument is "open" and you can climb to the top, ascending the internal staircase.

To return, go on beyond the monument to join a grassy path, the start of the zigzag way that brings you to a reinforced path at the foot of the steep bracken-clad slopes. Turn right and walk towards the town. Pass through another of the excellent gates. Go ahead along a wide walled track, Ladies Walk. At its end cross the entrance to the Hospice and stroll the continuing track.

This eventually brings you to the left of the parish church, St Mary's. Join Church Walk and go ahead to a crossroads, with a small roundabout. Cross with care to take the second right to return to The Gill.

Walk 36: Ulverston – Newland – Broughton Beck

Ulverston – Ladies Walk – Newland – The Falls – Mansriggs – Mansriggs Hall – Broughton Beck – St James's Church – Hollowmire – Stony Crag – Newbiggin – Windy Ash – Higher Lath farm – Bortree Stile – Old Hall farm – Gill Banks, Ulverston

Start/finish: As this walk will take over three hours, choose one of Ulverston's long stay-car parks. Theatre Street car park is a good place to start, giving you the opportunity to walk through the attractive market town and explore its alleys and cobbled streets (GR 288782).

Type of walk: This 7½-miler allows you to savour the peace and quiet of this lovely corner of South Cumbria. There is some walking over narrow roads but the way is mainly over pastures. Many stiles and gates must be negotiated. Approaches to farms can be muddy after rain. The views on the outward and the return route are delightful and will make you want to linger along the way.

Map: OS Outdoor Leisure 6 (new series). A very small section of the walk is to be found on the OS 7 (new series).

Nearest towns: Ulverston, Barrow-in-Furness, Kendal.

Public transport: Stagecoach Cumberland from Kendal, Barrow, Windermere, inquiries 01946 63222. North Western trains from Manchester, inquiries 0345 484950.

Refreshments/toilets: Ulverston.

In Ulverston's heyday many of the views from this walk would have been obscured by a pall of smoke from the numerous and varied mills in the town. It was once the most important town of South Cumbria, taking over after Dalton-in-Furness was ravaged by plague. Iron-ore from Newland helped to make Ulverston a boom town. But booms bust and Ulverston went into decline when the railway came and continued on to Barrow, a rapidly developing town which built more efficient furnaces and had a good port.

The Walk

From the parking area in Theatre Street, turn left and left again to walk along New Market Street. Cross Market Street and go ahead through one of Ulverston's intriguing alleys. Wind left to pass the Heritage Centre and go on to turn right onto Kings Street. At the mini-roundabout, cross and walk ahead along Church Walk. At its end, stroll on to the right of the church of St Mary with Holy Trinity. Enjoy the wide Ladies Walk as you progress. Go past the Hospice and walk on.

Just beyond a huge piece of limestone embedded in the path, go through the gate to walk the good reinforced track that skirts Hoad Hill. (For details of the Hoad monument, see the previous walk.) The view across Ulverston to the estuary is magnificent. Ignore any left turns and go on, gradually descending,

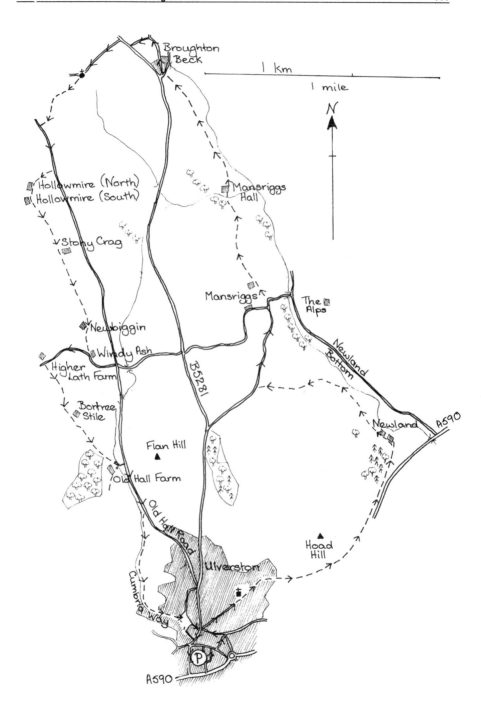

under trees, to pass through a kissing gate that brings you to the side of the A590.

Walk ahead on the wide pavement for 100 metres and then take a narrow road off left. When the barn of a farm at Newland lies ahead, take a reinforced track climbing steadily on the left. Go on up beneath deciduous trees to pass through a gate and along a grassy track. Enter more woodland and continue on a wide track, ignoring the path that slopes down on the right. Go through a gap and climb gently along a sunken track, shadowed by an arch of hedgerow trees. Follow the track as it winds left to pass through a gate. Go along the track, left, and then right to pass The Falls, following the waymarks directing to, and then up, the access road, with a fine view of the Lakeland peaks to the right.

On joining a tarmacked road, turn right, to walk on through pleasing undulating countryside. Ignore the left turn at Low Mansriggs and walk on a few metres to take a stile ahead at the point where the road swings right. With the wall to the left, walk ahead (keeping to the slightly higher ground, so that you remain above a very wet area), to a waymarked stile in the far left corner.

Beyond, go on to climb a small bank left, and then continue beside the dense hedgerow to your right. Go through a gate and take another, immediately on the right. Stride the reinforced way to pass through a gate to Mansriggs Hall farm. Cross the access track and press on, with the farm and its buildings to your right.

Go through the gate and cross the pasture to a gate in the bottom right corner.

Carry on through a boulder-strewn area, with Newland Beck away to the right. Pass through a derelict wall and then go on bearing left to walk beside a wall on your left. Climb a stile in the top left corner. Go on beside the wall on the left and walk on through a gated pasture. Descend towards the clearly visible telephone box at Broughton Beck.

Ignore the main road, the B5281, and walk the narrow lane that runs parallel with it. Just before the farm, climb a hedged track on the left to a gate which gives access to the busy road. Turn right and, with extreme care, walk a few metres. Cross when you can see your way clear, cut across the verge and take the quiet lane, signposted Netherhouses.

Stroll on to pass an attractive single-storey building, once the village school, which was built in 1770. Church services were held here and portable altar rails were brought out each Sunday. Beyond is Broughton Beck's St John's church. It was built in 1873 and from its doorway there is a dramatic view of Coniston Old Man. Turn left beyond the church, to walk a walled way. To your right is the house where the schoolmaster once lived. The old school and the schoolmaster's house are now private dwellings.

Beyond the gate, strike half right across the field to the far right wall to go through a wooden kissing gate. Continue on to the far right corner to go through a similar gate to join a narrow road. Turn left and walk on for 400 metres to take an even narrower right turn, which leads to Hollowmire farm (north). Follow the road round left and then obey the well signposted way to walk left in front of Hollowmire farm (south) to pass through the narrowest of gates.

Wind right to edge the hedge on your right, from where you can see Hoad monument peeping over the top of Flan Hill. Watch out for the easy-to-miss clapper bridge and a tiny gated stile through the hedge, on your right. Beyond go on in the same general direction to pass through a gate to join a track. Walk on to pass through a gate to the right of Stony Crag farm and almost immediately take another gate on the right. Stride on in the same general direction beside a short wall on your left.

Go on across the field, step across the beck and climb its shallow bank to a stile. Walk on to go through a step stile in the boundary wall and carry on through two more gates to join a narrow road at Newbiggin. Continue ahead to Newbiggin Hall, where you wind right and then left to go through a gate. Stroll ahead, along the bottom of the pasture, beside the wall to the left, to Windy Ash. Turn right onto a narrow road and climb for 400 metres. Pause often to enjoy the views into Yorkshire.

The steep ascent seems to go on and on but when you stand by the wall stile, opposite Higher Lath farm, the superb view of Morecambe Bay is a great reward for your effort. Once over the stile walk ahead to a stile marked by a tall post. Descend the clear way between hillocks. The next stile, which takes you over the next wall, lies slightly right, just left of a gate through the wall. Beyond step across a stream and descend to pass through two kissing gates to the right of a fine dwelling, Bortree Stile.

Descend to a stile to the left top of the corner of Old Hall Wood. Follow the narrow path downhill, with the wood to your right, and head across the pasture to the left of Old Flan Hall farm. Climb the step stile in the far corner, near to the beck, turn right and walk to the access track. Go left to join Old Hall Road, where you turn right. Stroll on for 400 metres to take, on the right, a kissing gate, signposted The Gill, $\frac{1}{2}$ mile.

Dawdle the clear way through a pasture, then woodland, with the beck to your right, to come to The Gill on the edge of Ulverston. Go on along one of the narrow roads to come to Kings Street, where you turn right. Cross the top of Market Street and walk on. The next left turn is Theatre Street.

Church at Broughton Beck

Walk 37: Broughton Beck

Broughton Beck – Bencragg Hill – Low Scathwaite – High Scathwaite –
Wood End – Lads Head – Lowick Beacon Knapperthaw – Broughton Beck

Start/finish: The village of Broughton Beck lies just off the B5281 between Ulverston (1 mile) and Gawthwaite (2 miles) on the A5092. Parking is scarce but there are two or three spaces beside the farmhouse in the centre of the village. The farmer is happy that you should park here but would like to be told that you are doing so.

Type of walk: A pleasing rarely-walked 6-miler through quiet pastures and woodland, and over delightful common land. For most of the walk the views of the Lakeland Fells are magnificent. The waymarking for the first half of the walk is excellent but does not continue once you have left Lads Head Plantation.

Map: OS Outdoor Leisure 6 and 7 (new series).

Nearest town: Ulverston.

Public transport: Postbus 523, Stagecoach Cumberland 01946 63222.

Refreshments/toilets: Ulverston, Broughton-in-Furness.

If you have parked by the farm, return to the phone box on the A5092. From here, walk left, the narrow lane that runs at right angles to the A-road, in the direction of Lowick Green. Cross the stone bridge over Broughton Beck and take, a few metres along on the right, the signposted step stile that decants you into a copse.

A stile in the right corner of the boundary wall leads you into a pasture. As you walk on, look right to see Ulverston's Hoad monument. Go on to climb two more stiles. Bear slightly left as you continue on the buttressed way to pass through two signposted gates. Before the next gate, which gives access to a

Bramble

track to Ben Cragg farm, turn left and ascend the fell, keeping to the left of Ben Cragg Hill, to a ladder stile over the wall.

Beyond turn left and edge the pasture to the far left corner and climb the stile. Descend the pasture to Low Scathwaite farm to take a signposted stile beside the gate. At the narrow road, turn left and follow it as it bends right and then left. Just beyond the next right turn, take the signposted stile set back from the road on the right. Walk ahead on a raised bank to a ladder stile in the wall on the right. Go on in the same direction with the wall now to your left to a stile, just before a gate, onto a road. As you go enjoy the undulating countryside all around and the magnificent view ahead.

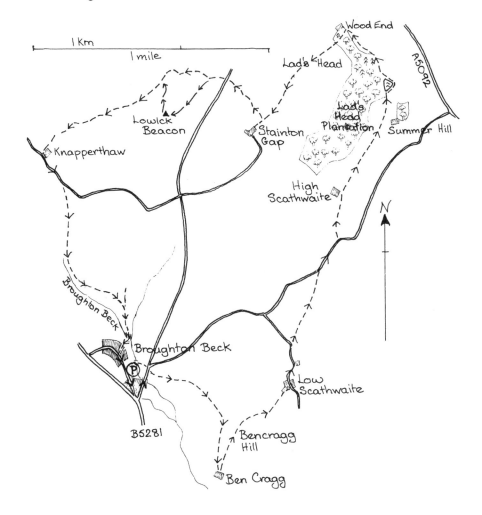

Walk on (right) along the road and, where it divides, take the left branch to High Scathwaite. Follow the waymarks through the tiny settlement and then on to a ladder stile. Ignore the paths that go left or right and walk ahead, and then slightly right, across the large pasture to a kissing gate in the fence. Continue on the same diagonal to a stile in the bottom corner beside the grounds of a large house named Summer Hill.

Once over the stile, walk the wide track and follow it right and left as it winds round a pretty ornamental lake. The route continues on its stiled way, keeping parallel with Lads Head Plantation on your left. Ahead is a dramatic view of the Coniston fells. At the lane, turn left.

Just before the dwellings at Wood End, take the signposted stile into the deciduous woodland. Climb steadily through the trees, as directed by the waymarks, to emerge onto Lads Head by a waymarked stile (the last waymark to be seen at the time of writing).

Continue uphill, through a tangle of bracken and bramble, picking your steps carefully to avoid wet areas after heavy rain, heading steadily right, to come close to the boundary wall. Where it turns away right, turn right with it and then, with the wall still to your right, strike away from it, steadily left. There are tracks of sorts, but no very clear ones. Aim for the top left corner (that is in a south-westerly direction). Once over the brow you will spot Stainton Gap farm – head towards it.

If you are on the right of way as you near the farm, you ford a narrow stream and then come beside the wall. This joins a cart track from the farm where you turn sharp right, with a wall to your left. Follow the track to a narrow road. Cross and continue up a wide grassy swathe through the bracken-clad slopes of Lowick Beacon. Continue steadily climbing, keeping the high ground to your left. If you wish to visit the cairn, take a narrower path leading left and straight up. The view is incredible.

If you have decided to leave your visit to the cairn to another day, keep on straight ahead to come to a wooden gate with a stone step stile to the right. (If you have swung slightly left and come to a metal gate, backtrack along the wall to the wooden gate.) Once through, turn left and keep beside the wall almost to the far left corner, where you take a rather rickety stone step stile over the wall. Beyond go on in the same direction to walk a walled way.

Press on along the delightful way and, beyond the gate, follow the track, downhill, to pass through the outbuildings at Knapperthaw farm. Turn left, onto the Cumbria Way, to walk a narrow lane. Go through a gate and as you begin to climb the slope, bear off right along a cart track to a gate. Beside it is a stone step stile and this is the way you continue.

Keep beside the wall on the right and climb the next stile. Beyond continue with the hedge to the right and carry on to another stile, which gives access to a path at the side of a hayfield, with Broughton Beck chuckling to the right. Climb the next stile and go on. Ignore the clapper footbridge and carry on to pass through a gateless gap. Climb the stile ahead and the next one and continue to the corner to take a clapper bridge over the beck. Walk on along the cart track. Bear right and then left to return to where you started your walk.

Walk 38: Colton

Farmer's Arms, Spark Bridge – Sayles farm – Bessy Bank Lane – Stock – Oxen Park – Colton – Tottlebank – Spark Bridge

Start/finish: A lay-by that is really a short stretch of old road, opposite the Farmer's Arms on the A5092 (GR 302850). This lies 1½ miles north-west of Greenodd.

Type of walk: This pleasing 8-miler, after a steep narrow lane climb, takes you along well waymarked paths and bridleways through the delightful undulating countryside that lies between the foot of Coniston Water and the Greenodd Sands. It goes by Colton church and Tottlebank chapel and several ancient inns. There is some road walking.

Map: OS Outdoor Leisure 7 (new series).

Nearest town: Ulverston.

Public transport: Stagecoach Cumberland, Windermere – Ulverston 518, inquiries 01946 63222. Alight at Greenodd and walk narrow road to Spark Bridge (see map).

Refreshments/toilets: At Spark Bridge, the Farmer's Arms and the Royal Oak. At Oxen Park, the Manor Arms Hotel.

Leave the lay-by by the west end and, with care, cross the often busy A-road. Go down the side road, passing on your left the Farmer's Arms. This dates from the 16th century and still has its spinning gallery.

Continue on downhill to pass the Royal Oak and, beyond, the remains of the

Footbridge near Colton

bobbin mill, which was closed in 1983. Go over the River Crake and take the second left turn. Climb the narrow lane and, as you take a pause for breath, look back to see the weirs on the Crake that provided the head of water for the mill.

Go on climbing to the brow and leave the lane by the signposted bridleway on the left, the second footpath going off left from this long steep lane. Follow the tractor track and, where it divides, keep to the left branch. Stroll on over upland pasture, which has scattered gorse bushes and rocky outcrops, keeping beside the wall on your left. Pass through the next two gates. Look left for a pleasing view of bracken-clad Lowick Common.

Follow the arrows directing you through Sayles farm, with the stabling to your left. Stride on the farm track and leave it left, at a waymarked post. Go on over a large rough pasture. Pass through a gate and continue ahead over another pasture, keeping to the left of the telegraph poles, to a signposted gate to Bessy Bank Lane.

Turn left and walk for 200 metres to take an arrowed walled track on the right and on to pass between the outbuildings of Hill Park farm. At the last barn follow the track left and then continue with it as it swings right and becomes pleasantly hedged. Go on uphill on the bridleway, ignoring a path that goes off left. Stroll on over another upland pasture to pass through the gate at the top of the slope and continue straight ahead to enter conifer woodland by another gate. Ignore any side turns and walk straight through the woodland.

Emerge onto a walled pasture that soon becomes a walled track. Go with the wall on your left towards Stock farm and the three-armed signpost before the dwelling. Here turn sharp right to take a footpath, signposted Abbot Park. The waymarks lead you by the wall on the left and then over a wet area to a stone stepped stile. Continue on, following the arrows to enter Park End wood. Drop downhill to cross a ride and go on descending to leave the trees by a gate. Stroll on beside a tiny stream, which you cross by a footbridge. Follow the waymark, directing you diagonally uphill to a gate in the wall on your right. Continue on the same diagonal to come to a gate to Abbot Park farm.

Beyond, join the metalled access track on the right and then leave it almost immediately, following the signpost on your left, which directs you across rough ground to a stepped stile in the wall. Continue over bracken and heather, still in the same direction, to another stile. Cross the corner of a pasture to the next stile and, beyond, follow the narrow path through bramble, bracken, heather and bilberry. Cross a wide ride and go on ahead (easy to miss the narrow path here) through the fell vegetation to come to the side of a wall on your left.

The narrow clear path then descends steeply through sapling birch to a bridleway. Cross this and bear right, taking the upper of two tracks. This leads to a footbridge over Colton Beck and then on to a road. Turn left to walk towards the delightful village of Oxen Park. At the triangle keep to the right branch to walk the exceedingly narrow way between the cottages, some dating from the 18th century, to the Manor Arms Hotel. Look for the house with the date 1679 on it and a wall sign of a blacksmith.

Continue along the road in the direction of Colton. After 400 metres take the

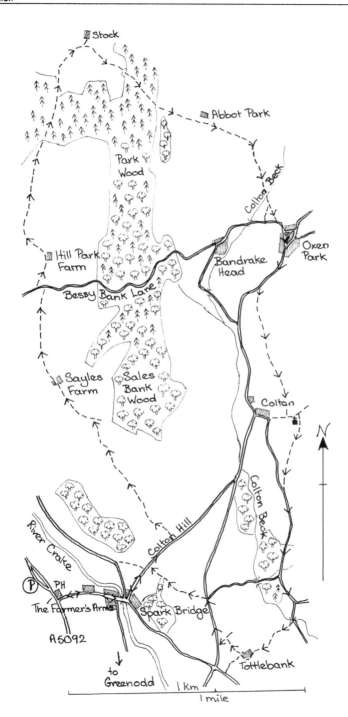

footpath on the left to the church (the signpost is obscured by a large hawthorn bush). The path keeps well up the slope but parallel with the road below. Look for the iron kissing gate as you approach the church, then continue beside the wall on your right to a fascinating kissing gate set between two huge slabs of slate. Go on, with the wall now to your left, to a modern kissing gate. The track beyond leads to the church.

Holy Trinity stands on the top of a hill above the hamlet of Colton. Across the track stands the church hall, once the village school. Enjoy the view of the fells from here, and then leave by the signposted footpath that runs above the church, keeping close to the wall of the graveyard. The way can get overgrown with gorse and bramble and cattle churn the soil. Keep to the left of a small pool and then descend (no real path) to a narrow road.

Turn left, pass Ridding Side farm and walk on for half a mile along the lovely gated way. Ignore the right turn and, where the road divides, take the right fork. Drop down the lane to cross Little Mill Bridge and take the signposted footpath on the right. This ascends through trees that have been coppiced in earlier years. Charcoal burners would also have worked the woods, the charcoal being used for iron making. Emerge from the trees by a gate, and bear slightly right to pass through a gateless gap in the hedge. Go on beside the hedge on your right and pass through a gate on the right. Walk ahead to another beside Tottlebank farm to join a narrow lane, which leads to the Baptist church. This was founded in 1669 and was built five miles from Ulverston, in accordance with a law of Charles II, which said that non-conformists could not worship nearer than that to a town.

Take the gate between the church and the graveyard and walk straight ahead to a kissing gate to a track, where you turn left. At the road, turn right and walk to the signposted gate on the left, before the next farm, Broad Hawes. Keep beside the wall on the right and follow the track until you reach the narrow lane taken at the start of the walk. Turn left and descend to Spark Bridge. Cross the Crake and climb uphill to the lay-by.

Juniper

Walk 39: Top o' Selside – Grizedale Forest

Dodgson Wood car park – Low Parkamoor – Top o' Selside – Set Level, Grizedale Forest – Penny Bank – Old Parrock Hill – Low Bethecar – High Bethecar – Selside – Low Parkamoor – Dodgson Wood

Start/finish: National Trust Dodgson Wood car park (GR 299927) on the east side of Coniston Water. From Coniston, it is the third car park on the left.

Type of walk: This is an exciting, challenging 8½-mile walk over heather moors and through a forest. The tracks and roads through the conifers of Grizedale make for easy, fast walking. There are clear paths to Top o' Selside and an intermittent path from the summit into the forest. The route from the top of Penny Bank to Low Bethecar, though a footpath on the map, is not at all clear and should not be attempted in the mist. From High Bethecar to Low Parkamoor the path should present no problems, except in the mist.

Map: OS Outdoor Leisure 6 and 7 (new series).

Nearest town/village: Ulverston, Coniston.

Public transport: None.

Refreshments and toilets: Coniston.

From the terrace-like track above Coniston Water you can look down on Peel Island. Arthur Ransome, journalist and author, called it Wild Cat Island in his famous "Swallows and Amazons" book, the first of his successful novels for children. Ransome spent his holidays at High Nibthwaite and the idyllic small hamlet, at the foot of the lake, was to inspire his many writings.

The Walk

Leave the small parking area by a reinforced track that bears gently right through fine oak woodland to a small National Trust barn. Keep to the right of it and wind round beside it. Follow the way to a stile beyond which a board asks you to follow the white arrows and markers along a permissive path to Low Parkamoor.

The grand track climbs steadily by gentle zigzags through the deciduous woodland. Step across a small stream and follow the curving way for a few steps. Don't miss the white waymark and painted arrow which, when the main track goes left, directs you right. Step across a second beck and go on along a narrow path through the trees, waymarked and with a fence to your left.

Ignore the gate on the left to come to an arrow directing you acutely left to a small gate through the fell wall. Continue upwards through the gill on a rough path, with a beck and a wall to your left. Scattered juniper, birch and holly cover the steep slopes to your right. Pause and look back, as you ascend, for your first glimpse of the lake.

Look for the three horizontal bars in the wall bridging the beck. This structure prevents sheep from straying into the small gill but gaps between the slabs allow water to pass through when the beck is in spate.

Then the way goes on along a grassy swathe, through bracken, to join a wide track. Turn right to stroll on the glorious way, with magnificent views over the lake and South Furness. Watch for Peel Island coming into view – it is soon obscured by the larches of Rigg Wood. After the track has dropped a little it begins to climb gently to a crest before it descends more steeply. Here, where you are opposite Peel Island now in view again, look for the unmarked track branching off left through bracken. After 30 metres take another grassy path, again on the left, to ascend the fellside. (If you miss this second left turn you'll walk your return route!)

Follow the clear winding path through bracken and heather. At a T-junction of tracks, bear left and go on through knolls and outcrops to reach the summit cairn, which remains hidden until the last moment. Enjoy the panoramic view, stretching from Black Combe to the Howgill Fells and out across Morecambe Bay. Pause to admire the attractive rush-fringed isolated Arnsbarrow Tarn below Arnsbarrow Hill – neither visited on this walk.

Head on along a narrower path, slightly east of north (leaving the tarn away to the right and behind you), aiming for a gate into Grizedale Forest. The path often disappears but when you can spot the gate into the conifers make a beeline for the fence to the right of it, so avoiding a small steepish gill.

Beyond the gate, walk ahead between sitka spruce. At the T-junction turn right to walk a forest road. Continue on to the next T-junction, where you turn right again. Walk on to a Y-junction to take the right branch. Two hundred metres along, look for an easy-to-miss narrow green path, going off left, to a hidden waymarked stile over the fence. Beyond go through bracken to the side of Bell Beck. Step across and climb steadily along a wide track, beside the ruined wall on your left and Penny Bank to your right. Follow the way, which soon becomes walled (ruinous), all the way to a gate onto Bethecar Moor.

Pause at the gate to get your bearings. The highest ground, ahead and to your right, is Old Parrock Hill. Go ahead, keeping slightly left of some miry ground. Step across Yew Beck and climb gently to pass to the left of the hill. Continue on to come to a fine cairn, set in a rough circle of stones.

From here you can spot the walled green pastures at Low Bethecar. Continue in that direction, high on the slopes and along a narrow path. It crosses the rough pastures and begins to descend towards a wet area in the valley to your right. Before you reach the mire take any of the clear narrow paths that keep to the higher ground on your left. Eventually you come near to the fell wall and you can see the stile right, passing through the wall, across the low lying ground. Step across the stream and climb the stile.

Follow the waymark directing you half right. The next waymark directs you acute right and along a grassy trod (a delight after the moorland intermittent path). This leads to a higher waymarked stile in the wall you have just crossed. Beyond, bear left and continue beside the wall on your left on a good path. Ignore the next waymarked stile in the wall (this gives access to High Bethecar) and continue on beside it. Pass an old rusty baler and walk on. Ignore a path on the right and climb gently up a small slope with the wall to the left.

Here a clear path swings away from the wall, right, across the moor. The

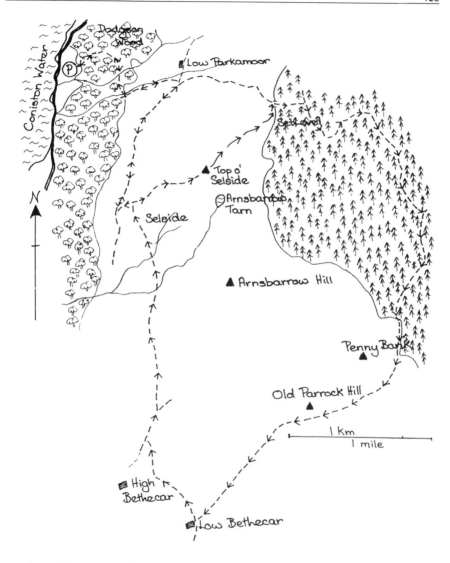

route continues on and on, crossing wet areas, climbing through rocky hillocks, but always remains clear and easy to follow. It continues for nearly 1½ miles and brings you to the wide terrace-like track high above Peel Island.

Turn right and retrace your steps towards Low Parkamoor. Watch out for the path descending just before the gill and well before the dwelling. Descend to the stile. Follow the well waymarked route downhill through the lovely woodland to the car park at the side of Coniston Water.

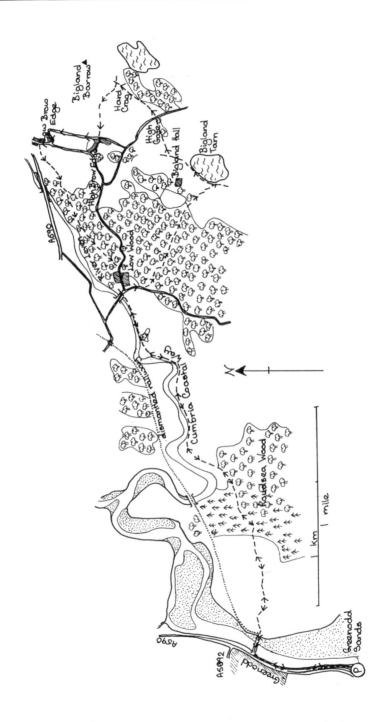

Walk 40: Bigland Tarn

Greenodd (Cumbria Coastal Way, CCW) – Roudsea Wood – Low Wood –
Bigland Tarn – High Gate – Hard Crag – High Brow Edge – Low Brow Edge
– Low Wood – Greenodd

Start/finish: Barr End car park, picnic area and fishing access, off the A590, south of the village of Greenodd, beside the Leven Estuary (GR 316816), three miles north east of Ulverston.

Type of walk: A pleasing 7-miler with good paths and tracks taking you across the Mosses, through Roudsea Wood (nature reserve) and beside the River Leven to Low Wood. Steepish 3/4 mile climb to Bigland Tarn, using a pleasing path through woodland. Then follows a short foray out onto the fell of Bigland Allotment. The return is made through more pleasant woodland beside the Leven to Low Wood. The outward route to here is used for the return.

Map: OS Outdoor Leisure 7 (new series).

Nearest town: Ulverston.

Public transport: Stagecoach Cumberland buses 518 and other various services. Inquiries 01946 63222.

Refreshments: Greenodd village, Ulverston.

Toilets: In car park.

Along the footpath, beside the estuary to the footbridge, is quite different from what it was in the 18th century. Then the shoreline was a port for transporting slate from Coniston and charcoal and iron from the many bloomeries nearby. Shipbuilding flourished along the water's edge and some of the staithes are still visible. With the coming of the railway, and the viaducts built across Morecambe Bay, all this busy activity was swept away.

The Walk

Return to the entrance of the car park and continue along the narrow path beside the fence. To your left hurries the traffic on the busy A-road to Barrow-in-Furness. As you near the road bridge over the River Crake, the path divides. Take the rising path (the left branch) and follow it onto the fenced path at the side of the A590. This leads you, well protected, to the start, on the right, of the fine footbridge across a wide tidal stretch of the River Leven.

Once over, go ahead on the Cumbria Coastal Way (CCW) to take a stile into a pasture. Climb the next stile and go on ahead to go through a gate. At the next gate take the stile to join a metalled road. Continue ahead along the delightful way. Ignore the left turn and stroll on through Roudsea Wood and then out into more pastures.

The narrow road then comes close to the Leven, beside which stands a sturdy fishing hut. Here anglers fish for sea trout, trout and salmon on their way upstream on the tide. The fish pass through Lake Windermere and then on into the mountain streams to spawn.

Go on beside the lovely river to cross a cattle grid. Beyond turn left over a drainage ditch. Walk ahead beside another delightful stretch of the river to go through a kissing gate. Stroll on, edging a wide loop of the Leven to another gate. Walk through a small copse, still beside the river, to pass through a gate to a metalled road.

Stride on ahead to the edge of the hamlet of Low Wood. At the crossroads, turn right and walk with care along the B5278. Cross at a safe place to take the signposted CCW on the opposite side of the road. The narrow stony path climbs steadily through deciduous woodland. Pause regularly to enjoy the plant and bird life. At a wide track, cross and continue upward as directed by the signpost. Go on up and up to a gate to pass out of the trees to a pasture. Walk ahead following the waymarks to come to the side of the lovely tarn.

Great crested grebe

Pause here and enjoy the tranquil pool, where you might see great crested grebes, mallards, coots and goosanders. The tarn and the nearby Bigland Hall are set in a hollow in the top of the hill you have just climbed and cannot be overlooked – a useful asset when the site was first settled in Norse times.

Continue beside the tarn in a clockwise direction, with the house hidden beyond banking, to come to a metalled right branch. Cross the cattle grid and stride the narrow way to come to High Gate and a narrow road. Cross and take the footpath opposite, signposted Hazelrigg.

Walk ahead to pass through a gap in the wall. Follow the path as it climbs gently through outcrops, which in August support great banks of sweet smelling heather. Enjoy the glorious views. Look for a signposted stile in the wall on your left, just before a pretty reedy pool. Take the stile and walk across the rough pasture to a difficult-to-spot rickety stile in the bottom left corner. Beyond, swing left to a gate and a continuing walled track, in the bottom left corner.

At the road, turn right and remain on it to descend through High Brow Edge.

From here you can see Backbarrow and the steam train puffing through the woodland about the Lakeside and Haverthwaite railway. Continue downhill and, just before Low Brow Edge, take the signposted public bridleway on the left.

At the end of the metalling, go on along a delectable green lane into decidu-ous woodland above the River Leven. Stroll on the lovely way to pass part of the old gunpowder works.

This produced, between the late 18th and 19th centuries, blasting powder for quarries, and for copper, coal and lead mines. The vast woodlands around Low Wood supplied the silver birch and alder charcoal needed and on the lower slopes of the fells grew juniper, an ingredient of gunpowder.

The River Leven supplied the water power to drive the machinery and through the nearby small port of Milnthorpe other essential raw materials ar-rived and finished products were transported to Liverpool.

At the end of the path, turn right onto a road and walk ahead through Low Wood. Look right between the cottages to see the main gunpowder works, now housing a crystal engraving firm. At the junction of roads, cross and con-tinue on the tarmacked way walked earlier. Look for the stile on the right that gives access to pastures beside the river, now on you right.

At the road, turn right to walk the delightful way to pass through Roudsea Wood. Continue until the road makes a sharp left turn and retrace your steps across the pastures to the bridge. At the bridge end, turn left to walk the narrow path to regain the starting point.

Walk 41: Rusland – Satterthwaite – Grizedale Forest

Blind Lane – Force Mills and Falls – Rusland church – Force Forge farm – Grizedale Forest Visitor Centre – High Dale – Breasty Haws – Satterthwaite – Blind Lane

Start/finish: Small parking area north-east of Force Mills (GR 346914). Take the B-road south from Grizedale Visitor Centre towards Satterthwaite. Continue to Force Mills and turn left. The car park is on the left. It can also be approached from the A590.

Type of walk: This is a 9½-mile roller-coaster walk that takes you through much of the deciduous woodland of Grizedale Forest. It is a pleasure to walk at any time of the year, full of birdsong in spring, a riot of colour in autumn and sheltered during windy or stormy weather. Good paths take you easily through the woodland, but as this walk follows rights of way rather than waymarked forest trails the map listed below is a great help in finding the route. The walk is long but not strenuous – the paths have easy gradients and surfaces are generally good.

Map: OS Outdoor Leisure 7 The English Lakes, south eastern area. Note the 'P' indicating the parking area is printed on the wrong side of the road.

Nearest town: Ulverston, Bowness-on-Windermere.

Public transport: Stagecoach Cumberland, Ulverston to Grizedale. Summer services Barrow to Ambleside and Far Sawrey to Ambleside. Inquiries 01946 63222

Refreshments: Visitor Centre.

The delightful Rusland Valley lies between Lake Windermere and Coniston Water. It was once owned by the monks of Furness Abbey, who farmed it and operated "bloomeries" – that is, hearths for smelting. The secret valley is criss-crossed by narrow roads, which present tourists with a map-reading test.

St Paul's Church occupies a rocky prominence, with a grand view of the vale. It was much loved by Arthur Ransome, of "Swallows and Amazons" fame, who is buried in the churchyard together with his wife Eugenia.

Grizedale Forest Park is managed by Forest Enterprise, part of the Forestry Commission. The charcoal burners' hearths, once so busy, have long since gone cold and the bloomeries fallen silent, but the forest still provides for the needs of industry. Every day five lorries leave laden with timber. It has an interesting visitor centre and many miles of paths and tracks.

The Walk

Turn right out of the parking area and walk to the T-junction at Force Mills. Continue ahead and take the unmarked byway on the left. Go on along the walled and hedged track and follow it through woodland. Pass through the gate and, remaining on the track, continue through larch and oak, until you reach a minor road, where you turn right to walk to Rusland Church. Go inside to view its plain simplicity and then return to the gate by which you entered.

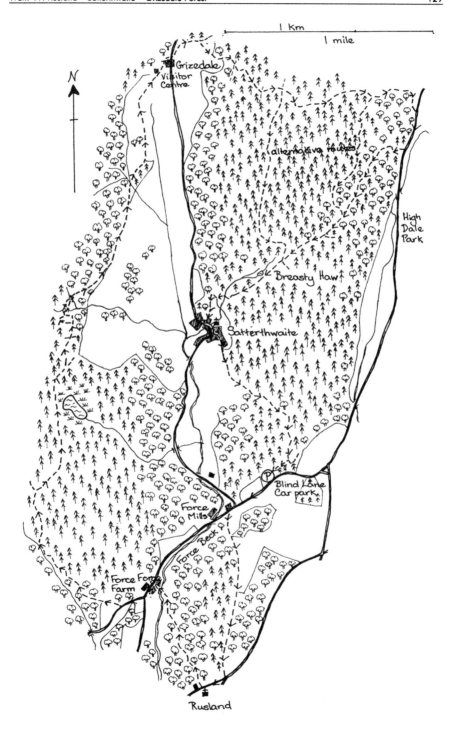

Rusland

Cross the road and climb the stile opposite into the grassy surround of the reading room. Take the stone stepped stile on the right to join a path that climbs steadily through woodland. Stroll on along the clear way until you reach a waymark directing you left. Cross a footbridge over the tumbling Force Beck and follow the footpath to the road at Force Forge farm, where you turn left.

Walk the hedged road, and then continue along a narrower walled one that goes off right. Continue to a gated track on the right, signposted Bethecar Moor and Satterthwaite. The track, which soon becomes a path in a groove, passes under young beech, beside outcrops of rock and climbs deep into the forest. Continue on slightly left, ignoring the grooved way as it swings off right and becomes blocked with debris.

As you ascend look for hard fern lining the way, each with tall fertile fronds growing upwards. Then to the left you see a hurrying beck, and to the right a tree-clad hillock.

At the T-junction of tracks, turn right. As you continue enjoy the pleasing view over a small tarn. Carry on and, at the next T-junction, turn left. Ignore a crossing of narrow paths, to take, on the left, a path marked with green banded posts that cuts off a corner of the road and leads to an isolated picnic table and shelter. The footpath then zigzags downhill, delectably so, returning you to the forest road once more. Here you have a choice, either to continue on the road or to take the meandering footpath that goes off to the right of the road, a short delightful diversion, over bridges and through leafy glades to eventually rejoin the forest road.

Hard fern

Walk on until you come to the edge of the forest, with pastures to the right. At a Y-junction of tracks take the right branch to go over a cattle grid and descend towards the visitor centre, nestling in its hollow.

Turn right to pass through the farm and stroll left just before the huge wall of the centre. Look for the pretty rusty-backed fern, which grows between the stones of the wall, and then walk on into the centre. Here you will wish to dawdle and enjoy the shop and the cafe. There are picnic tables and toilets and there is an exciting adventure playground.

Cross the B-road from the centre and take the rough track ascending acute left. As you reach an unusual sculpted seat on the left, take the gate opposite, on the right. Walk through a high pasture, with a wall to the right and a pleasing view down into the valley. Follow the wall round as the way bears right and brings you to a stile into the forest.

Ascend the slope to step across a stream. Cross the forest road and go on up a stepped rock to follow a waymarked path that goes on up, bearing slightly left. The way passes through conifers and then joins another forest road. Turn right and then, almost immediately left, to pass through a tall deer gate and walk a glorious path through heather, bracken, young birch and many outcrops.

Continue beside the wall and follow the next waymark that directs you left, with a view of Claife Heights over the tops of trees. Go on through banks of heather and then through a "passage" of deciduous woodland to pass through another tall deer gate to join a forest road. Notice the sculpted bat by the gate.

Cross the road (if you turn right along this forest road it will shorten the walk to Satterthwaite – see map) and take a waymarked bridleway opposite, which soon begins to descend steadily. Cross a small stream and continue descending, ignoring any paths off to reach another forest road, which you cross (if you turn right here this will also shorten your return to Satterthwaite – see map). Go on downhill to reach a minor road, where you turn right to walk the quiet way through the secret valley of High Dale.

Remain on the road, ignoring the bridleway off left, to take, just beyond on the right, a wide track. This well graded way climbs steeply uphill through more woodland. Eventually it begins to descend a little and crosses a tiny stream before passing into a conifer plantation. Cross a forest road (this is the second forest road you may have taken) and continue on a blue banded path. Walk ahead and begin to descend on a good path into more woodland.

The blue banded way leads to another forest road (the first short-cut you may have preferred to take), which you again cross to follow the waymarkers, downhill through deciduous woodland. At the road, turn left to walk the narrow lane into Satterthwaite (thwaite, Norse for a clearing in a forest). Visit the parish church of All Saints, with its diagonally placed south-west porch close to the tower. Then turn left beyond it.

Follow the narrow lane to the edge of the village and bear left into a bridleway, when the minor road begins to descend. Follow the track as it gradually veers right through yew, holly and oak and, then climbs steeply with a wall to the left. Where the path divides keep to the right fork to cross a wide forest road. Continue down the narrow path to join the forest road again. Turn right and follow it as it curves steadily downhill. Watch out for the white banded footpath going off right and follow this to return to the car park.

Walk 42: High Dam – Finsthwaite Tower

Finsthwaite – Low Dam – High Dam- Finsthwaite church – Wintering Park – Newby Bridge – Summer House Knott – Finsthwaite Tower – Finsthwaite

Start/finish: Small parking area, pleasingly sited north east of the village of Finsthwaite (GR 368882). It is easy to drive past the access lane because it is indicated on the B-road only by a footpath sign; the 'P' sign stands a short distance up the access lane. Finsthwaite can be approached either from Newby Bridge or Hawkshead.

Type of walk: This 4½-miler is one of the loveliest in the Lake District. Good paths take you round the delightful tarns. The walk from Finsthwaite to Newby Bridge is over parkland, followed by a steady descent to the valley, all well waymarked. The climb to Finsthwaite Tower, though unrelenting, is through deciduous woodland, a joy to walk at any time of the year. A new path opened Easter 1999, takes you easily to its junction with the wide grassy trod coming up from Lakeside. This leads you back through more fine woodland to Finsthwaite.

Map: OS Outdoor Leisure 7 The English Lakes, south eastern area (new series).

Nearest town: Bowness-on-Windermere.

Public transport: Stagecoach Cumberland, summer service only – Finsthwaite, Lakeside, Grange, Cartmel, inquiries 01946 63222.

Refreshments: Newby Bridge.

In 1835 Finsthwaite Tarn was dammed to create a reservoir for the bobbin mill at Low Stott Park, which needed water power. A series of streams and culverts carried water across Finsthwaite Heights and down through the trees to power a large water wheel. This in turn powered the machinery in the mill. By 1858 the water wheel had been replaced by a water turbine. This required constant water pressure and a second dam was constructed.

The higher tarn, High Dam, is surrounded by open heather-clad fells, with rocky outcrops. Lower down, wetter soil originally supported peat bog. From the 1850s this was planted with oak and birch to provide coppice woodland for charcoal burning for the mill. Since 1973 this delectable area has been owned and managed by the National Park Authority.

The Walk

Turn right out of the parking area and climb steadily to a gate. Beyond, go on up through woodland, remaining beside the beck, to join a good track through oak and birch. Once through a kissing gate, take the left branch and go on along a buttressed path to come to the first dam, with the pleasing pool spread out before you. Follow the path that keeps to the right side of the small stretch of water and cross footbridges over feeder streams.

Go on to the extensive upper lake. Turn left to cross the dam to begin your clockwise stroll. Follow the path right. Ignore the left turn to Rusland and continue high above the water, with bracken and heather on either side. Sit awhile on the well positioned seat and enjoy this lovely corner of Lakeland.

Continue your circuit of the lake and retrace your outward route, passing both dams and continuing to the kissing gate once again. Remain on the path

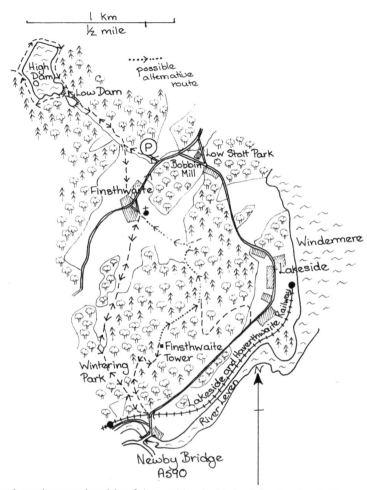

and, when close to the side of the rushing beck, look for the footbridge across it and a kissing gate beyond that gives access into sloping pastures.

Descend, bearing steadily right, to a small gate just past two green holiday homes. Beyond, stroll beside the wall on the right and, near its end, cross the pasture to a waymarked gate between cottages at Finsthwaite. Walk the alleyway to a gate to the road, where you turn right. Take the next left to approach St Peter's church.

In the churchyard is a plain cross depicting the burial place of the "Finsthwaite princess", who was believed to be the natural daughter of the Young Pretender.

Take the signposted gate opposite the church and walk ahead on a clear path, over stiled pastures (with no instructions needed), to a stile into the deciduous woodland of Wintering Park. Follow the clear path that goes down and down and brings you to a gate to a track close to Newby Bridge. Stride this for 100 metres then take the footpath on the left, signposted "Finsthwaite Tower".

Climb steadily a narrow reinforced footpath between fencing which takes you into more magnificent woodland, high above Newby Bridge. Pass through a gate and go on up. Follow the way as it winds right and is stepped. The path, narrower now, leads you to a viewpoint, a small grassy patch surrounded by rocky outcrops.

Leave this high place by a narrow left turn (easily missed) to join a continuing clear path that takes you on through the trees. Suddenly, ahead, romantically, stands the tower. Climb the short path to its foot. Look for the plaque above the entrance door. It says, "the tower was erected to honour members of the Royal Navy whose conduct and valour decisively defeated the fleets of France, Spain and Holland". Beneath the inscription is the date, 1799.

Rejoin the main track and continue on until you reach the point where it makes a wide curve left. Here bear steadily right along the waymarked path. This takes you easily through the woodland to join the track coming up from Lakeside. Turn left and follow the sylvan way to come eventually to the edge of the trees. Go on slightly right for a short distance, turn left and take a stile into a pasture. Walk ahead towards Finsthwaite church over the stiled fields.

Join the narrow road, go past the church and follow the road as it bears right. Continue on to pass the last house of the village and take the narrow lane, climbing left, to the car park.

Low Dam, Finsthwaite

Walk 43: Cartmel

Cartmel Racecourse – Low Bank Side – Birkby Hall – Templand –
Allithwaite – High Fell Gate – Spring Bank – Hampsfield Fell (Hampsfell
on signposts) – Hospice – Pit farm – Cartmel

Start/finish: Park and start at Cartmel Racecourse, (GR 378787) where you are asked to use an honesty box. Cartmel village lies 4 miles south of the A590 and can be approached from Haverthwaite or south-east of Newby Bridge. Once you are in the village, the racecourse is well signposted.

Type of walk: This 6½-mile walk takes you through lush gentle pastures around the delightful old village. As you go there are fine views of Morecambe Bay. There is easy walking for much of the way but woodland paths can be muddy after rain. Take care over the deep grooves (grykes) of the limestone pavement.

Map: OS Outdoor Leisure 7.

Nearest towns: Kendal, Ulverston.

Public transport: Buses from Barrow and Kendal, Stagecoach Cumberland, inquiries 01946 63222. North Western Trains from Barrow or Carnforth, alight at Cark and Cartmel station, join walk at Low Bank Side, inquiries 0345 484950.

Refreshments/toilets: Cartmel.

Legend says that Cartmel Races were founded by the monks of the Priory as a treat for Whitsun. Not so long ago the grandstand was removed and stored away each year, but today the course is permanent. The patron of the races is Lord Cavendish, who owns the land on which they take place.

The Walk

Set off from the end of the car park, furthest away from the village. Stride ahead on the wide cart track, with deciduous woodland never far away. Enjoy the undulating landscape, with lush hedgerows beneath which, in spring and summer, grow a plethora of wild flowers.

Go on the gated way to pass through mature woodland. At a Y-junction, keep to the right branch to ascend gently under an avenue of sycamore and beech, where the woodland floor can be a blaze of pink if the foxgloves are in flower. Pass through a gate and go on along a metalled track. Continue climbing steadily and at the brow of the slope you have a fine, extensive view of Morecambe Bay.

Just before the next gate turn left and, keeping beside the wall on the right, continue to a stepped stile which gives access to a small deciduous wood. Walk on to pass through a squeeze stile into coniferous woodland. Drop down through the trees to a stile to a farm track at Low Bank Side.

Cross the track and walk ahead along the farm's access track to cross Mere Beck just before you come to the side of the B-road from Cark. Cross and take the stone-stepped stile, slightly right, signposted Templand via Birkby Hall. The path takes you gently uphill beside a large field. At the corner bear right and

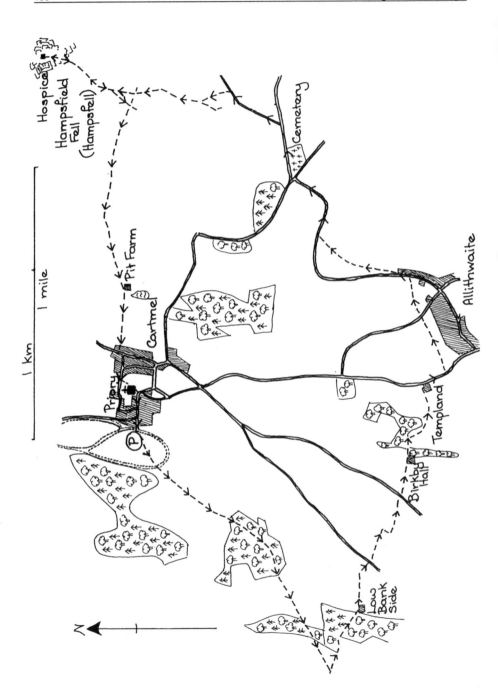

walk on to take an unsignposted field gate on your left. Beyond, walk ahead with the hedge to your right and a pleasing view of the Priory away to your left.

At the narrow lane, cross and, slightly right, take the footpath signposted Allithwaite. Saunter up the lane to Birkby, where you bear left as directed by an arrow. Follow the way right and then right again to walk a narrow walled and hedged track that is difficult to spot if the vegetation is luxuriant.

Swing left at the end of the narrow track and then follow the path as it bears right to ascend through trees to a gap stile into a pasture. Go straight ahead to a sturdy gap stile at the top of a bank between the end of the wall and some trees.

Head on along the narrow path through a hay meadow towards some buildings. Well before these be alert for the gate and stile on your left, at the end of the path. Carry on beside the hedge on your right, with a dramatic view of the Lakeland tops to your left, to join a lane.

Turn right and, after 100 paces, take the tarmacked lane, signposted Grange and Lindale, on your left. Pass Templand farm (1687) on your left and look for the well beyond. A notice says that it was probably sunk in the late 15th century. At some point in time it was capped and remained so until it was rediscovered in 1994.

At the lane end, cross and, a few paces left, take the well constructed stile and walk ahead through two pastures, with the wall to your left, to join another lane. Here turn left and walk on to come to a strategically placed seat on the left. After a pause, take the stile just beyond on the right.

Turn left and stride the rough pasture, climbing steadily, and bearing right away from the lane. Look here, in summer, for rock rose, bedstraw and wild thyme flowering. An unsignposted gate, with a stone stepped stile beside it, gives access to the lane. (This route over the rough fell has enabled you to cut off a large corner of the lane.)

Turn right and follow the pleasing way as it swings left, and continues to a junction of busy roads. Cross the road ahead, wind left and then right round the boundary of the cemetery and walk the right turn for Grange-over-Sands. Use the grassy verge as you go with the cemetery to your right. Pass Grange Fell golf club on your left and, just beyond, take a quiet lane on the left.

Enjoy the magnificent view of the bay as you climb steadily. At the brow and by a signpost, with directions for a footpath on the right, go through an unsignposted gate on your left, onto the glorious limestone fell. Bear right, heading towards a wall. Continue beside it, gently ascending, until you reach a gate and a stile through the wall.

Beyond, stride the wide grassy way. On either side are bracken, scattered hawthorn and limestone outcrops. At the junction of tracks, keep to the left branch, with the telegraph wires to your right. Stroll on to another junction of paths, from where you can see the hospice on the fell above. From here the stiled route to it, over layers of limestone, is clearly waymarked.

Go inside the hospice and sit on the seats provided by Mr Remington of Longlands Hall, a 19th century pastor, and read his delightful poems inscribed high on the walls. Then climb the outside steps to enjoy the panoramic views and use the indicator placed there by a retired railwayman nearly a century later.

Limestone scar, Hampsfell

Descend from the hospice and return along your approach route. At the first waymarked post, take the right fork. At the next one, turn right to descend over the slopes, down and down, to a tall kissing gate with glorious views ahead.

Once through, strike across, left, to a gate adjacent to Pit farm. Follow the signpost, which stands beyond, in the direction of Cartmel. Keep beside the hedge to your left to go through a tall wooden gate. A ginnel brings you to a lane. Turn left and then right to come to the gate, on your left, to the church. The Norman edifice dominates the picturesque old houses that cluster around it. Perhaps you have time to go inside and enjoy its wonderful atmosphere, its magnificent carvings and the moving memorial tablets set in the floor.

Continue on through the village's lively square, with its pump and fish slabs. Look back to see the church's two towers, one set diagonally to the other. Look also for the fine gatehouse and then walk left of the post office to return to the car park.

Walk 44: Flookburgh

*Flookburgh – Sand Gate – Canon Winder – Cowpren Point – Old
Embankment – West Plain farm – Holme – (Humphrey Head) – Wyke
farm – Allithwaite – Boarbank Hall – Applebury Hill farm – Flookburgh*

Start/finish: Flookburgh's large square, once the site of an old chapel and graveyard
(GR 367758). To reach the village leave the A590, in a southerly direction, for
Grange-over-Sands or Haverthwaite, and then follow the signs for Flookburgh.

Type of walk: An 8½-mile walk (10 if you visit Humphrey Head) with lots of contrast.
The start is around Lenibrick Point and Cowpren Point, and these are best attempted
when the tide is out. Then follows a glorious stroll along the Old Embankment. Some
unavoidable road walking next, much of it along a narrow lane. The path through
meadows to Allithwaite is pleasant indeed. Then follows another short and narrow
road walk, which can be quite busy. The final stretch is through meadows on
Applebury Hill and makes a charming climax to a good stroll. Before you start your return you may wish to extend the walk to visit Humphrey Head, a magnificent limestone promontory extending into Morecambe Bay.

Map: OS Outdoor Leisure 7 (new series).

Public transport: Stagecoach Cumberland 534 Finsthwaite, Newby Bridge,
Flookburgh, Grange-over-Sands and Cartmel, inquiries 01946 63222. North Western Trains, Barrow – Manchester, alight at Cark. Inquiries 0345 484950.

Nearest town: Grange-over-Sands.

Refreshments: In Flookburgh.

Toilets: Well signposted from the square.

---

*Roads from Flookburgh's square lead to the shore. Tractor wheel marks
criss-cross the sand, where fishermen, who once used horses and carts, still follow the tides for flukes, shrimps and cockles. It was an important stopping place
on the ancient crossing routes over the sands, which connected Lancaster with
Furness.*

*Many ships came to fish the mussel beds close to Sandgate but this ceased when
the building of the railway caused silting in the estuary. Land south of the village
was once all sand and very high tides were known to wash over the streets of the
village. But now the sea is a mile away, and half a mile of this walk takes you
along a straight road over the reclaimed land.*

The Walk

Leave the square by Main Street (west), following the signpost for "Sandgate
and The Shore". Look for several 17th century houses lining the way. Climb the
hill out of the village. At the brow, the houses are left behind. A grand view of
the estuary lies ahead and to the right you can see the Lakeland mountains.
Continue to the shore and turn left to walk the signposted Cumbria Coastal Way
(CCW)

A narrow path leads along the shoreline and here you should see much bird

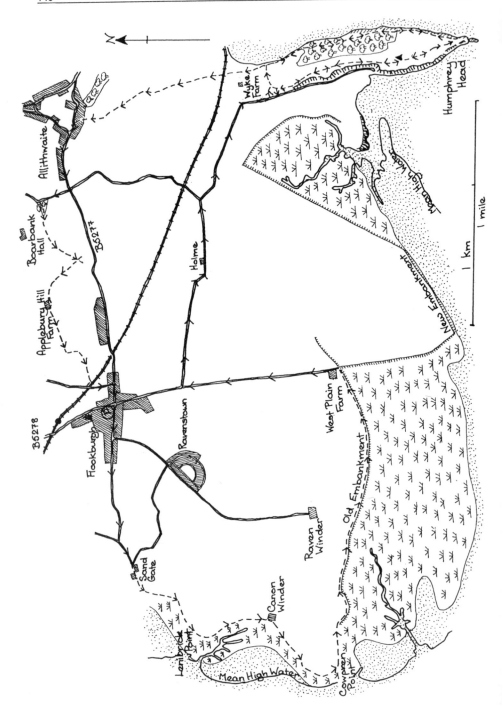

life. Follow the path as it winds round Lenibrick Point to come to a stile. Walk on beside a sturdy wall to the next stile. Beyond this, the path continues, keeping parallel with the wall to pass close to the outside of Canon Winder farm. This fine building is so called because it once belonged to the canons of Cartmel Priory. Further inland is Raven Winder farm, named after a Scandinavian. Both farms are said to have halls of great antiquity. They are now part of the Holker estates.

Go on along the path. Some parts are wet where cows have puddled the ground. Make full use of the stones and timber placed there by other walkers. And then climb a small slope to go on along the top of the Old Embankment.

Enjoy this pleasing way from where, stretching seaward, you can see cattle grazing the salt marshes, which in places look like a permanent fine lawn. Inland you can see Ravenstown, a crescent-shaped area of houses. These were built for the staff of a naval aerodrome towards the end of the 1914-18 war. The site took the name from the farmstead of Raven Winder and the roads are named after wartime battles.

At the end of the raised way, turn left to join the very straight road that crosses reclaimed land – still on the CCW. Half a mile along, turn right to walk, for just over a mile, a narrow hedged lane (still the CCW) that passes through quiet countryside, where you pass a house named Holme. Ignore a left turn to Allithwaite and follow the narrow way to come to a left turn into a walled and hedged track (Still the CCW).

Here you might like to make a diversion to walk on Humphrey Head. The 45 metre cliffs rise steeply from high tide mark and are the only ones of any size between St Bees Head and North Wales.

To enter the nature reserve, walk on to take the next left turn and follow the path over the impressive cliffs to reach the finger of rocks that project into the bay. Walk round the point and wander across the unimproved flower-rich grassland and small areas of heath. Finally return to the road. To continue the walk, turn right and continue to the walled track now on your right.

Climb the pleasing way and once over the brow of the track, you see ahead, a fine expansive view of the bay. Gently drop down to the shore, turn left and walk the narrow, and sometimes wet, path edging a vast salt marsh. Keep a solid limestone wall to your left. Look out for the sturdy stile in it and follow the instructions to take another on the right, both keeping you away from Wyke farmhouse.

Pass under the railway bridge and then stride through the pastures, keeping straight ahead from one stile to the next, to arrive at Allithwaite. The village is believed to have been founded by the Vikings. Join the B5277 and go left. Walk with care along the narrow busy road for a quarter of a mile to take, on the right, a steeply ascending narrow lane. Continue beside a copse on the left to go through a metal kissing gate, on the left, at the edge of the wood.

Pause here to look right to see Boarbank Hall. Here in the last century lived a Miss Mary Lambert, a benefactress who bequeathed money for the building of St Mary's church, Allithwaite, and the vicarage, schoolhouse and school.

Boarbank Hall is now a convent, guest house and nursing home run by Augustinian sisters.

Once in the meadow, turn left immediately, to pass through a stone gap stile into the copse. Follow the narrow path through the trees to climb two walls by sturdy through steps. Join a narrow access road and walk right for a few steps to where it makes a sharp bend. Behind a very large tree, on the left, stands another metal kissing gate, which is easy to miss.

Cross the pasture to a limestone gap stile and then head right over a hillock. Look for a small gate, to the left of a farm gate, well to the right of a clump of conifers on another hillock. Beyond, cross the pasture and then skirt left of the outbuildings of Applebury hill farm, passing through two gates. Beyond, turn left and walk down the pasture to an ingenious stone stile to the right of a gate. Stand here and look back to see a fine lime kiln to the left of the farm.

Carry on, keeping beside the hedge on your right. Ahead you can see Flookburgh's parish church of St John. At the hedge corner, bear left to continue along the side of the pasture to another excellent stile. Beyond, walk ahead along a raised way to join a quiet road, Green Lane, where you turn left. Pause on the bridge as you go over the railway line for another good view of the fine church.

Walk to the road end. Cross Market Street, and go right to pass the Manor House, built in 1686, which stands almost opposite the Crown Inn. Go on into a small square to see a market cross. Opposite is the Hope and Anchor Inn. Continue on to where you have parked.

Humphrey Head

Walk 45: Low Newton

Low Newton – High Newton – Barber Green – Field Broughton – High Cark
– Seatle – Ayside – Height – Tow Top Road – Back o' th' Fell Road – Dixon
Heights- Buck Crag – High Newton

Start/finish: A large parking area outside Yew Tree Barn (which sells architectural antiques), Low Newton. The barn lies on the west side of the A590 just north of where it ceases to be a dual carriage-way (GR 403823). Just over 2 miles north is Lake Windermere.

Type of walk: This pleasing 7½-miler takes you through the delectable countryside on either side of the intrusive A590. West of the A-road quiet narrow lanes, hidden hedged tracks and easy-to-follow paths take you through secluded pastures and woodland. To the east, you go by a picturesque reservoir high up on open fell, along a widish road and then descend steeply by one of Cumbria's narrow lanes to the Winster valley. The return over Dixon Heights lies through dense scrub and trees but has been waymarked, so you should have no difficulty finding your way – though the arrowed posts are rather short and might be difficult to spot when the bracken is at full height. There are many stiles to climb on this walk and some were made for people with very long legs. Two or three have no posts to help you to balance and extra care should be taken on these.

Maps: OS Outdoor Leisure 7 (new series).

Nearest towns: Kendal, Grange-over-Sands, Bowness-on-Windermere.

Public transport: Buses from Barrow and Kendal, Stagecoach Cumberland, inquiries 01946 63222.

Refreshments/toilets: Yew Tree Barn.

From the parking area walk north for 100 metres along the grass verge of the busy road and turn left into a loop of the old road. Take the stone-step stile on the left, where the signpost is obscured by a large bush. Walk ahead, with the wall to your left, to a waymarked stile. Go ahead to climb the next stile and then bear right across the corner of the pasture to a very narrow gap stile. Such stiles are known as a "fat man's agony" – this one is even a thin woman's agony.

Walk straight across the pasture to a slightly wider gap stile and then ahead again to another. Go on through a wall gap and then on to a hidden kissing gate to the right of a metal gate, to join a walled track. Pass through a gate into the picturesque village of High Newton, where you turn left. As you go look for the 18th and 19th century wall plaques on its fine houses and cottages.

At the T-junction, turn left and then, just beyond the houses, turn right, following the signpost for Barber Green. Walk the pleasant walled lane with pleasing views of the estuary. Go on ahead at the crossroads to pass, on your left, five huge yew trees. There were once seven. Legend has it that a sea captain was given the farm, and the Spanish yews, for service to his king - but no one seems to know which king.

Stroll on past the tiny oval green on your left and go on a few steps to take the next left turn. Beyond the first house on your right, take a stile. Go ahead to take the waymarked gate, the left of two. Walk ahead to a step stile in the wall. Beyond walk ahead to the next gap stile, to be found in the far left corner. Press on, with a very wide wall to your left, to a stone step stile in the wall beyond. Stroll on to a grey metal gate set among outbuildings to the right of Greaves farmhouse.

Turn left to walk the narrow lane in front of the house to take the signposted way on the right. Go on beside the wall on your right to pass through a wall gap. Continue ahead with the wall now to your left. Climb the difficult stone step stile in the corner. Saunter on, with the continuing wall to your left. Go right of the farmyard and then follow the clear waymarks to a gap stile to a narrow lane, where you turn right.

Dawdle the pleasing way in the direction of Field Broughton church. Watch for the moment when you have a dramatic view of the red tiled building with its fine spire, crowned with a weathercock. It was consecrated in 1894 on the site of an old chapel, which was demolished in 1892. The money for the new church was provided by Harriet Margaret Hibbert, who wished it to be built in memory of her husband, but she died before the church was completed.

Continue down the lane to the lych gate to the church, which you may like to visit. In January the churchyard is full of snowdrops.

At the T-junction turn left and walk on for 200 metres and take a right turn to walk beside a piece of common land. Here stands the village pound, used for hundreds of years for holding sheep that had strayed. Bear right to pass in front of two tiny cottages and to join a track. Cross Ayside Pool, which once provided Cartmel Priory with their fish, and go on the hedged and gated track.

At the end of the track, climb the stile on the right and head across a pasture to the far right corner. Once over, walk with the wall to your left to join another superb walled track. Beyond the gate, go on ahead (ignore the left turn) and saunter on to join a narrow road at High Cark.

Turn left, continue by the farm and descend the hill. Just before the farm, High Cark Hall, take a track on the right, signposted Seatle. Go on until you come to a small barn on your right, just before a road. Here take the stile adjoining the barn. Head across the pasture towards a small wood to a hidden stile that lies well to the right of a gate. Stroll through the fine oak trees (no clear path) to its far side to a stile, which gives access to a pasture.

Stride straight ahead to a stile to a road. Turn left and walk 100 metres to a stile on the right, signposted Ayside. This is another difficult stile. Walk ahead to a stile through a short stretch of wall. Stroll on beside the wall on your left to a well constructed gate in the corner. Climb the steepish slope and take a stile on the left. Beyond, bear right and walk down beside the wall on your right to join a track that takes you into the attractive hamlet of Ayside. Once clogs and shoes were made here.

Cross the A590 with great care and continue up the narrow lane opposite. After 100 metres take the signposted gate on the left. Climb the sloping pasture, gradually moving away from the wall on your left. Cross the narrow Belman Beck and walk ahead towards the fence at the side of the road. Turn left and follow the narrow path, uphill, beside the fenced road. Climb the stile onto the road, then continue ascending through the high walled pastures.

Over the wall to the left lies one of the High Newton reservoirs. Pause at the end of the wall to look at this extensive stretch of water, which is edged with

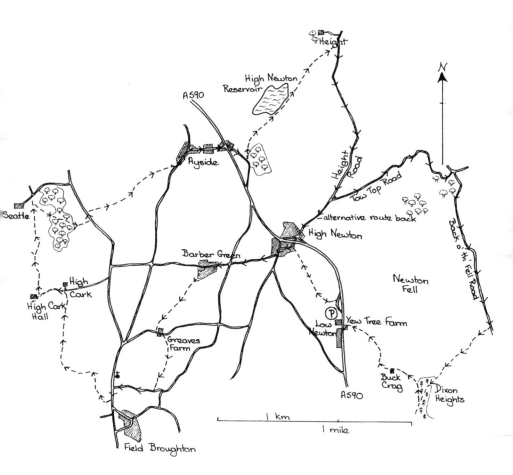

trees and fell slopes and on which a variety of duck swim. Go on to the gate across the road, with the sturdy house called Height to the left. Here turn sharp right to walk Height Road. Look left down over extensive plantings of conifers to Witherslack. Beyond lies the Kent estuary, silvered and sparkling.

At the T-junction you have a choice. You can continue on Height Road to descend quickly to High Newton and return by the field paths taken at the start of the walk; or you can turn left into Tow Top Road to continue the walk, following the signpost directions for Witherslack.

Ahead, as you go, you can see Yewbarrow and Whitbarrow Scar. Enjoy the quiet way that descends down and down, winding first left and then right to reduce the gradient. It passes through pastures patchworked with walls and punctuated with dramatic rocky outcrops. As you descend towards the Winster valley look away left to see Helton Tarn. It has long been believed that the first iron ship to float lies on the bottom of this reedy pool. It was built by the great ironmaster of Lindale, John Wilkinson (1728-1808), and was the prototype that ousted wooden ships. He also built iron bridges – and an iron coffin for himself.

At the crossroads, turn right in the direction of Lindale, to walk the tree-lined Back o' Th' Fell Road (OS map spelling). Look for tree creepers and long tailed tits as you walk the next mile. Go on past a barn on the left. Just beyond a metalled lane on the left, look for the footpath sign and stile on the right, beside a gate, which you take.

Walk straight ahead to the first waymark and begin your climb up the fell. At each waymark look ahead to see the next one. Pause often as you climb and look back for an incredible view of the Winster Valley below. In a lonely hollow, high up, you come to the side of the delightful Tom Tarn, below Dixon Heights. It is fringed with yellowing grass.

Climb the step stile in the wall to your left and stand at the top to see where the wall bisects the lovely pool. Beyond, walk by the side of the pool, passing through an large patch of gorse to come to a wide track. This runs at the side of extensive woodland, and there is a boundary wall to your right. The track is muddy at first but soon becomes a delight to descend. As you go look up through the fine beech on your left to see a splendid crumbling arched folly. Above stand the remnants of an old tower, but this can be seen only later on the walk.

Carry on down and down, remaining on the track, until you reach another coming in on your right, along which the walk continues. Follow the good track beside the wall on your left and below the tree-clad slopes of the towering Newton Fell. Climb another awkward stone-step stile and go on through bracken and scattered birch to pass to the right of the house at Buck Crag. Press on beside the wall and follow it as it climbs a little and then becomes a wide grassy track leading to the gate to Yew Tree farm.

Beyond the gate, walk the track as it makes a semi-circle round the outbuildings to join the A590. With care, cross and turn right to rejoin your car.

Folly, Dixon Heights

Walk 46: Gummer's How

Parking area – Gummer's How – Parking area

Start/finish: Gummer's How car park (GR 390876).

Type of walk: A good path, half a mile in length, followed by some easy scrambling, takes you to the top of this shapely fell.

Map: OS Outdoor Leisure 7 (new series).

Nearest town: Bowness-on-Windermere.

Public transport: Lakeside to Fell Foot, Windermere Lake Cruises, summer only, inquiries 01539 531188. Then walk up Fell Foot Brow.

Refreshments/toilets: None on route.

NB: You may wish to combine this walk with number 47. If so, cross the road from the kissing gate at the foot of Gummer's How, and take the gate opposite. Climb up the slope to join a wide track coming from the car park on your right. Turn left.

Gummer's How (1,054ft/321m) is the fine fell that lies to the left of the road from Fell Foot to Kendal. From the kissing gate, high on this road, the ascent to the top is barely 400ft/120m but from its rustic trig point you can enjoy dramatic views of the major Lakeland fells, the Howgills, the Pennines, Morecambe Bay and the Crake and Kent estuaries. From a point 100 metres to the north-west of the cairn you can see the full length of Windermere.

Cairn on Gummer's How

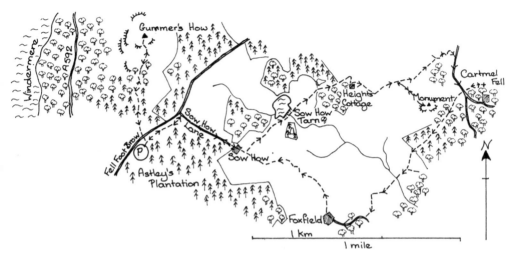

The Walk

From the car park, set in a clearing on the edge of Astley's Plantation, cross the road and walk a few yards to the right to take the kissing gate, which gives access to a good path. The steadily climbing way goes on through birch, sallow, rowan, beech and ferns, with glimpses of the lake to your left.

Enjoy the continuing well pitched stone stairway, which climbs straight up through rocky outcrops and heather. Look for Esthwaite Water coming into view. Then follows some fairly easy scrambling and, about 20 minutes after leaving the parking area, you reach the delightful summit.

Return by the same route.

Walk 47: Cartmel Fell

Gummer's How car park – Astley's Plantation – Sow How Lane – Sow How Tarn – Height's Cottage – Cartmel Fell Church – Foxfield – Sow How Lane

Start/finish: Car park in a clearing on the edge of Astley's Plantation near the brow of Fell Foot Brow lane (GR 390876).

Type of walk: A very pleasant 4½-miler on good paths across pasture and fellside, with magnificent views all the way. A visit to the lovely wayside church is a must for all.

Map: OS Outdoor Leisure 7 (new series).

Nearest town: Bowness-on-Windermere.

Public transport: See walk 46.

Refreshments: Newby Bridge, Bowness.

NB: To combine this walk with the previous one, cross the road from the kissing gate at the foot of Gummer's How and take the gate opposite. Walk ahead, up the slope, to join the wide track from the car park, where you turn left.

St Anthony's, tucked in a remote fold in the fells – so remote that first-time visitors have difficulty locating it – was built about 1504. It served the hill-farmers and their families who lived at least seven long miles from Cartmel Priory. But bodies still had to be taken to Cartmel for funerals until the chapel was granted burial rights in 1712. It is a plain, low, long church with perpendicular mullioned windows, a tower and a porch, the latter believed to be an Elizabethan extension.

The Walk

Leave by the north-east end of the car park (with Gummer's How to your left) and walk on along the way through the forest. As you go you meet a narrow path coming up the slope, from the road, on your left, and this junction is the point where walk 46 and the present one join.

Dawdle on along the needle-strewn track through mixed woodland to a stile in the boundary wall. Turn right to continue along the pleasing Sow How Lane, from where you look across rolling pastures. Pass between the buildings at Sow How farm and walk on to the signpost, which directs you left through park-like meadows. Go through a gate and follow the good track into scattered oaks. Pass, to your left, the delightful Sow How Tarn.

Cross the stream that emerges from the tarn and head up the grassy slope towards a waymark. Follow the path as it swings right along a diverted bridleway. Go through a gate into deciduous woodland and then out again along the path as it swings sharp right towards Heights Cottage. It then bears left and goes on between walls, with Scots pines and rhododendrons to your right.

Beyond the next gate stroll the track and go with it as it bears left as a wide grassy way. From here you can look towards the Howgills sprawled along the skyline. Continue until you can see a monument, across the pasture, and walk right to visit it. Sit in the seat that is set into a fine cairn to enjoy the glorious views of Scout Scar and Cunswick Scar and much of the Lyth valley. A plaque describes the monument as a ziggurat.

Return back across the rough turf to the grassy track and continue downhill to a gate. Beyond, a signpost directs you right, to zigzag downwards to the road. Turn right and walk the quiet lane to a signpost for Cartmel Fell. Turn in this direction and take, immediately on your left, a signposted footpath through bracken. This leads you to a very narrow squeeze stile into the churchyard of St Anthony's.

Go inside to see the large enclosed pews on either side of the knave. Look for the three-tiered pulpit; sermons are still preached from the highest level. Puzzle over the opening at floor level in the north-east corner – it is a "bole" and once had a wooden shutter. It was used to push debris and floor sweepings out of the church.

Before leaving this delightful Cumbrian corner, sit on the long stone bench outside and enjoy the peace. Here many years ago spectators sat and watched archery practice in the churchyard in the days before burials took place there. Parish meetings, too, were held here when the weather permitted.

Leave by the same gap stile and walk the footpath to the signpost. Cross the major road and climb a tall ladder stile opposite. Stride on, ignoring the narrow path up to the monument, and climb steadily to a tall gated ladder stile. Stroll the narrow path beyond, through young deciduous woodland. Pass through a gate onto a grassy path. It leads to a reinforced grassy track, where you turn right.

Pass through scattered alder, birch and bracken to cross a pretty stream. Go on through the next gate to walk a wide walled track. Follow it as it swings sharp left, as directed by an arrow. From here there are more stunning views. Beyond the next gate, join a very narrow lane to walk right. Continue on the pleasant way to pass through the tiny hamlet of Foxfield. Beyond, the metalled road goes on as a track and climbs to a gate onto open fell.

Stride the continuing track, now with a good view of Gummer's How. The gated way returns you to Sow How farm, passed through on your outward way. Go on along the quiet lane, almost to Fell Foot Brow lane. Turn left to climb the stile into the plantation and press on ahead, with more delightful glimpses of the lake as you go. The track ends at the parking area.

Sow How Tarn

Walk 48: Whitbarrow Scar – Foulshaw Moss

Derby Arms – Bull Bridge – Mill Side – Buckhouse Wood – Raven's Lodge – A590 – Foulshaw Cottages – High Foulshaw – Low Foulshaw – Crag Cottage – Main Drain – A590 – Derby Arms.

Start/finish: The old road below Latterbarrow (GR 442827). To reach this parking area take the side turn off the A590, signposted Witherslack. Once past the Derby Arms Hotel, turn left.

Type of walk: This 8-mile walk is full of contrasts. First, all is tranquillity as you pass through larch along a sheltered track, deep in pine needles, beneath Whitbarrow's flaring White Scar. After crossing the ever-busy A590 the walk follows the Cumbria Coastal Way (CCW), winding around Foulshaw Moss on a narrow, almost traffic-free road. It continues below the embanked River Kent and then along the top of the embankment to continue round Birkswood Point. The return route heads inland through quiet pastures on a narrow road to return to the start.

Map: OS Outdoor Leisure 7 (new series).

Nearest town: Grange-over-Sands.

Public transport: Stagecoach Cumberland, Kendal to Barrow, inquiries 01946 63222.

Refreshments: Derby Arms.

Walk back towards the hotel, cross the Witherslack road and continue ahead along the pleasantly hedged old road. After just over half a mile, leave it at the second signpost on the left, which directs you up a track towards Bull Bridge. Pass through the kissing gate on the right, just before a farmhouse. Beyond, continue ahead over a pasture, following the waymarks, to pass through a gate between a house and its outbuildings. Bear right and follow the track as it swings left to the road at Mill Side.

Cross and take, a few yards to the left, a signposted track up the fell. Pass through the farm buildings, where an old pump stands beside the way. Go through the waymarked gate to take another into Buckhouse Wood. Climb steadily a narrow path that joins a wider way coming in on your left. Walk right. Where the track swings right in front of a cottage, go ahead along a broad grassy way beside the walled woodland on your left, following the signpost directions.

Continue above Whitbarrow Lodge. Look right for an extensive view over the estuary. Then the way comes close to the foot of the sheer face of Whitbarrow and begins its long gentle descent. Pass through the gate to a narrow road. Turn right and continue to the side of the A590, where you turn left. Walkers with children or dogs should proceed with care along this 350 metre stretch of grassy verge.

Remain on the same side until you are opposite the narrow road signposted Foulshaw. Cross the dual carriageway, with great care, and go on along the quiet road. The metalled way takes you through well cared for pastures, where sheep graze, and on past Foulshaw Cottages. Notice as you go the very deep,

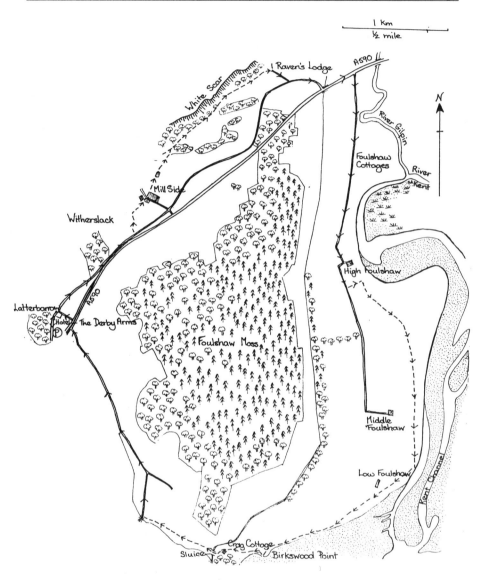

well maintained ditches, which drain the mosses. The main reclamation and consolidation took place in the 1850s when the Ulverston and Lancaster railway was completed.

The straight, virtually traffic-free road goes on with the embanked River Gilpin to your left and the huge conifer plantation of Foulshaw Moss away to your right. Before the trees were planted local people cut their peat here.

Pass High Foulshaw farm, where the path to the side of the embankment has been diverted for just over 200 metres further along the lane. Go through the gate on the left, cross the pasture to the next gate and turn right beside the high fenced embankment. Beyond it lies the River Kent, which has by now received the waters of the Gilpin.

Follow the way as it winds right beside a copse to pass through a kissing gate. Beyond, steps lead up to the top of the embankment, from where you can enjoy a dramatic view of the estuary over an intervening meadow. The way goes on and on. Ignore the access track to Low Foulshaw farm. Soon you will be able to spot the Kent viaduct, strung out across the estuary.

Across the Milnthorpe Sands you can see the white houses of Sandside and, behind, the huge quarry. Listen as you go for curlews calling and watch for swans, greylag geese and cormorants flying up the estuary. Go through the kissing gate at the end of the grassy swathe beside the embankment and walk on, over a pasture, to join a reinforced track. This continues behind Birkswood Point, where gorse is generally a mass of yellow blossoms.

Just beyond lies a large bay on the shore of which are convenient outcrops for a picnic. The leaflet promoted by South Lakeland District Council on the CCW reminds walkers that here there are quicksands, unpredictable deep channels and fast running tides. So this is a place to sit and enjoy the vast expanse of water or sand, depending on the tide, without venturing out.

Follow the track as it curves away from the shore and comes to the side of Crag Cottage. Ignore the sturdy bridge to the right over the Main Drain and the continuing road to Ulpha farm, and go on for 50 metres along the track. At the two armed signpost, walk right, still on the CCW, to cross a stile onto a narrow footbridge over a sturdily constructed sluice. Beyond, bear left to walk the footpath that runs parallel to a drainage ditch, now on your left. Go on over several pastures to reach a stile, which gives access to a minor road.

Turn right to stroll inland, passing between lush flat green fields, the way neatly bounded by well trimmed hedges. Notice as you go how some of the ditches have been reinforced two or more metres down. Ahead is a magnificent view of Whitbarrow Scar and you can just see the woodland, where you dawdled earlier on your walk.

Just before the A590, turn right and then left, as directed by the waymark, to pass under the A-road, and continue on to walk in front of the Derby Arms. The next left turn will return you to your car.

Cormorant in flight

Walk 49: Levens

Levens Bridge – Levens village – Brigsteer Park – Park End farm –
Holeslack farm – Sizergh Castle – Heaves farm – Levens church – Low
Levens farm – River Kent – Levens Bridge

Start/finish: Park in a large lay-by on a branch of the A6 north of Levens Bridge (GR 497854).

Type of walk: This delightful 5½-mile walk takes you through the rolling pastures and deciduous woodland close to Sizergh Castle. There is some walking along quiet roads. The tracks through Brigsteer Park and over nearby pastures are clear to follow and easy to walk.

Map: OS Outdoor Leisure 7 (new series).

Nearest town: Kendal.

Public transport: Stagecoach Cumberland, Kendal-Arnside, Kendal-Barrow, Windermere-Grange-Kendal, inquiries 01946 63222.

Refreshments and toilets: None on route. During the summer months you might wish to visit the pleasing gardens of Sizergh Castle (admission fee) and enjoy their teashop.

From the parking area, walk north along a narrow path to take a track on the left, signposted Levens. Follow the wide track to cross the bridge over the A590. Walk ahead to the next ladder stile and, beyond, follow a clear path across the pasture to a gate in the top left corner, close to the edge of Levens village. Once through the gate walk ahead to the road, where you turn right.

Continue ahead to go through the centre of the village, passing the bus shelter and the village shop on your left. Take the left turn here, to descend. Go by the Methodist Church, built in 1891. Cross the road and go on downhill, bearing steadily right. Continue on in this northerly direction, with glimpses through the houses on the left of the Lyth Valley. Before it was drained it was a forested area. The valley, or mosses, was where, for hundreds of years, villagers each had their own strip from which to cut peat. On the opposite side of the wide flat valley rise the dramatic slopes of Whitbarrow.

Beyond the semi-detached houses at the end of the village, and before farm outbuildings, turn left. Follow the track as it goes on to wind right to come to a signpost directing you to Park End. Stride ahead along the reinforced track and, where it swings left; take a kissing gate into deciduous woodland.

Goldcrest

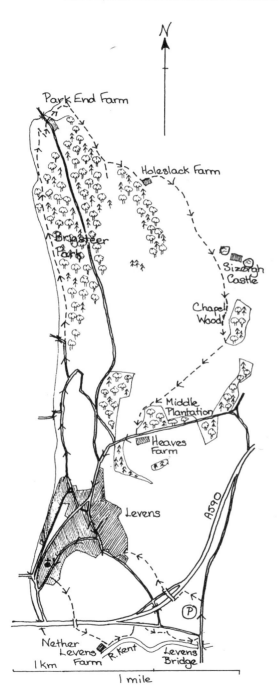

N

Park End Farm

Holeslack Farm

Brigsteer Park

Sizergh Castle

Chapel Wood

Middle Plantation

Heaves Farm

Levens

A590

Nether Levens Farm

R. Kent

Levens Bridge

1 km

1 mile

A distinct level path takes you through this ancient wood, rightly famous for its wonderful show of daffodils in spring. Once the trees were coppiced. Go quietly on your way, where you might see goldcrests slipping through the brambles or other low-growing vegetation.

Emerge from the trees by a kissing gate and follow an indistinct green swathe to zigzag up the grassy slope to a signposted gate in the top left corner, which gives access to a narrow road. A few metres along to the left is the picturesque farm of Park End.

Cross the road and go through the gate opposite, following the signpost for Brigsteer Brow. Pass through a small gated yard, between outbuildings, and take the next gate. Climb uphill, bearing left, to steps to a gate in the top left corner. The way continues on a reinforced walled track that is steep to climb. Follow the lane as it winds right. It leads you out onto a pasture to join another grassy track continuing on above the woody bank to your right. The track ceases soon after it has swung left. Bear right here and go on over the pasture towards the signposted track ahead.

Walk right along the reinforced way and follow it as it swings left to pass through a gate. The quiet remote track leads to Holeslack farmhouse. The fine dwelling snuggles in a hollow, with woodland at its back. From its front, it has a wide view over the pastures to Sizergh Castle. Just beyond the last wall on the right, climb the easy-to-miss stile to take a narrow footpath, steadily descending through woodland. It continues to a stile that returns you to the track from the farmhouse, by a large outbuilding.

Go on along the continuing track in the direction of the castle. Beyond the next gate a good track takes you to a second gate to the side of the castle. The core of the dramatic building is a 14th century pele tower, later extended. It contains some exceptional Elizabethan carved chimney pieces.

Turn right and, ignoring the stile to your right, stroll through the car park, keeping to the right side of it.

Just before the cattle grid on the exit road from the car park, turn right and stride ahead with the wall to your left. Go through the kissing gate and saunter on. Look over the wall to see a most attractive shelter beside the fenced Chapel Wood. Go through the next kissing gate and bear right to dawdle across a large pasture. The clear path brings you to a waymarked stile near the top right corner. There are more grand views of Whitbarrow ahead.

Follow the path in the same general direction to come to a gate in a wall beside Middle Plantation. Beyond, bear left, soon to climb a gap stile to the right of a large gate to join the road, with Heaves farm on the other side. Turn right to walk into Levens village. Go past the post office on your left and walk through the centre of the village. Beyond, take the right turn to come to a small triangle of grass, with the church on your right.

St John the Evangelist was built in 1828 by Mary Howard of Levens Hall after she had a disagreement with the vicar of Heversham, to which parish the village had originally belonged. The grey stone church has a fine pointed spire and this stands out as a striking landmark.

Opposite the church take a track, signposted Nether Levens. It passes between cottages to a stone stepped gap stile that is often obscured by parked vehicles. From the foot of this stile stride, half right, across the pasture. Use the ladder-stile to the left of a gate to join a concrete track. Follow this left to re-cross the A590 on a footbridge and continue to Nether Levens farmhouse, built in the 16th century. It stands on the bank of the River Kent and has some fine chimneys.

Turn left beyond the cattle grid to walk beside the river. Keep a lookout for kingfisher, dipper and mallard. Follow the track to the A6 slip road. Turn right and, 100 metres along, climb the stile on the right into a fenced path, with the road and hedge to your left. Walk on to take a ladder stile into more deciduous woodland. A good path takes you beside the river and to Levens Bridge. Cross the road with care to return to your car.

Walk 50: Milnthorpe – Heversham

Milnthorpe – Dallam Tower Park – Milnthorpe Bridge – Marsh Road – Marsh farm – College Green – Leasgill – Heversham – Heversham Head – Woodhouse lane – Haverflatts Lane – Milnthorpe

Start/finish: Park Road pay-and-display car park, Milnthorpe (GR 496815). Turn west off the A6 onto the B578 at the traffic lights in the middle of the village. The east turn, the B6385, leads to the square, where there are toilets and where you alight if travelling by bus.

Type of walk: An easy 6-miler which takes you, first, along quiet lanes across Milnthorpe Marsh. It then continues to Leasgill and Heversham, both of which nestle below Heversham Head. After you stroll the glorious turf of the high parkland, the way takes you over gently rolling pastures to Haverflatts, where you descend to Milnthorpe.

Map: OS Outdoor Leisure 7 (new series).

Nearest town: Kendal.

Public transport: Stagecoach Cumberland bus service from Kendal, Lancaster, Carlisle, inquiries 01946 63222.

Refreshments: Milnthorpe, Heversham.

The Athenaeum, the village hall, was founded as a reading room in 1872 by Frank Argles. The Argles family helped with the restoration of the parish church of St Peter, provided a new site for the village school and supplemented the village water supply. St Peter's church, believed to be more than a thousand years old, had a major restoration between 1868 and 1871. It has wide aisles, a fine beamed ceiling and some attractive stained glass. In the porch of the magnificent north door is a late ninth-century cross-shaft. Heversham Head has wonderful high level sloping pasture from where you obtain grand views of Morecambe Bay.

The Walk

Turn left out of the car park and walk, with care, on the narrow pavement to the second signposted footpath on the left. Cross the stone footbridge and go through the deer gate. Bear right to walk beside the River Bela, where you should pause to look back at the ancient cut-waters of the bridge. On the river a variety of ducks disport. About the pasture you might see a herd of fallow deer that roam freely over Dallam Tower Park.

Continue ahead to another deer gate and beyond walk right along a minor road to the often busy B-road to Arnside. Turn right to cross the fine single-span bridge and then go left along Marsh Road. This narrow, very straight way takes you out into the fertile pastures of Milnthorpe Marsh. As you go notice the drainage dykes, deep, straight and clear of debris, that have been cut to drain the one-time marshland.

To your left stretches a long embankment, separating the pastures and the road from the tidal River Kent, which once must have regularly overwhelmed

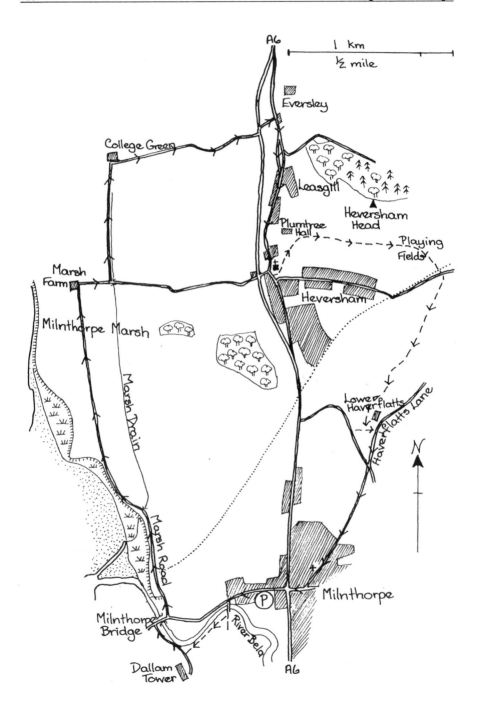

A6

1 km
½ mile

Eversley

College Green

Leasgill

Heversham
Head

Plumtree
Hall

Playing
Fields

Marsh
Farm

Heversham

Milnthorpe Marsh

Lower
Haverflatts

Haverflatts Lane

Marsh Drain

N

Marsh Road

Milnthorpe

Milnthorpe
Bridge

P

River Bela

Milnthorpe

Dallam
Tower

A6

the marsh. Ahead you can see Whitbarrow and the Furness Fells. To the right, across the pastures, the village straggles parallel with, and above, the A6, which by-passes it.

At Marsh farm, walk right to come to a small bridge over the Main Drain. Do not cross but turn left and continue on to the end of the road. Go right here to pass College Green and stride on to the side of the A6. Cross with extreme care and go on up a narrow lane to Leasgill. To your left, almost hidden by trees, stands Eversley House where the Argles family lived.

Turn right to walk between the delightful cottages, from where you have a dramatic view across the flat pastures and out to Morecambe Bay. At the Y-junction take the right branch to walk an even narrower lane to come to the village hall founded by Frank Argles. Rejoin the wider road and walk on to pass Plumtree Hall, where lived another benefactor of the village. Look on the left of the road for the village pump

Stride on to visit the striking church. Look for the huge parish chest, believed to date from about 1400. It is the only piece of furniture to survive a fire of 1600. It was used as a strongbox by parishioners until 1900. It is the largest and oldest chest in Westmorland. Opposite the church is the picturesque village store and post office.

Leave the church, but not the churchyard, and look for the gate in the north wall. It is obscured by vegetation and lies to the right of the old village school. Follow the good path uphill to a wall corner to go through a gap stile. Climb a few steps and continue to the next gap stile. Still climbing, take the kissing gate on the right. Go on uphill for a few more steps and then bear right to stroll for 650 metres across the glorious turf of Heversham Head. Keep parallel with the gardens of the houses below to your right and the wall, often hidden from view, to your left. Look for the rugby posts on playing fields below to your right and descend gently to a small gate in the enclosing wall. Go straight across to go through a gate, which gives access to a dismantled railway. Join a narrow road, turn left and take a signposted stepped gap stile on the right.

Beyond, bear steadily right to the top corner to go through a very sturdy stone stile. Go on beside the hedge on the left, with a spell-binding view ahead. Go through the gap stile at the corner of two hedges. Turn right and climb the ladder stile ahead. Turn left to continue towards Lower Haverflatts. Keep to the right of the dwellings and, beyond, pass through a gate in the hedge on your left. Walk across the pasture towards a tall wooden signpost to go through a gated stile in the hedge (difficult of access when the vegetation is flush) to join a very narrow lane.

Turn right and walk to the crossroads. Cross straight over and continue gently down an equally narrow lane, signposted Milnthorpe. As you go look right to see St Anthony's Tower, a folly, set on a small hillock. Go on into the village. Turn left to walk through Milnthorpe's largest square, brooded over by St Thomas's church, with its blue diamond-shaped clock.

Continue to the traffic lights, cross and walk on with care to turn left into the car park.

Walk 51: Milnthorpe – Beetham

*Milnthorpe – Dallam Tower Park – Milnthorpe Bridge – River Bela and
Milnthorpe Sands – Crow Wood – Haverbrack – Beetham Fell – Slack
Head – Beetham – Dallam Tower Park – Milnthorpe*

Start/finish: Park Road pay-and-display car park, Milnthorpe (GR **496815**). Turn
west off the A 6 onto the B578 at the traffic lights in the middle of the village. The east
turn, the B 6385, leads to the square, where there are toilets and where you might
alight if travelling by buses

Type of walk: This enjoyable 5½-miler takes you beside the River Bela to where it
flows out over Milnthorpe Sands. Then the walk continues inland, steadily climbing
through limestone pastures to the woodlands of Beetham Fell. This is followed by a
descent to the charming village of Beetham and then a one-mile stroll through the
lovely parkland of Dallam Tower, with its magnificent herd of fallow deer.

Map: OS Outdoor Leisure 7 (new series).

Nearest town: Kendal.

Public transport: Stagecoach Cumberland bus service from Kendal, Lancaster,
Carlisle, inquiries 01946 63222.

Refreshments/toilets: Milnthorpe.

---

*Milnthorpe, which sits astride the A6 between Kendal and Lancaster, has been a
market town since the 14th century. Once it was a small port for Kendal but its
use declined after the building of the Glasson Branch of the Lancaster Canal
when trade was transferred to Glasson. The port became redundant in 1857. The
final blow was the construction of the Arnside viaduct for the Ulverston and Lancaster railway, which caused silting and changes in the Kent estuary.*

*Delightful Beetham village, 1½ miles south of Milnthorpe and to the west of the
A6, lies in the vale of the River Bela. The fine towered church of St Michael and
All Saints is well worth a visit. Beyond it, on the road to Slackhead, stands the
black and white Wheatsheaf Inn. Both buildings, and the picturesque cottages
surrounding them, nestle against rising woods to the west.*

The Walk

Turn left out of the car park and walk down Park Road. Take the second signposted footpath on the left to cross a delightful stone footbridge, with ancient
pointed cut-waters facing both up and downstream. It was built in 1730 and
takes you over the River Bela. Go through the iron kissing gate, which is twice
the usual height to keep the fallow deer in the park. Bear right to walk beside the
river and towards the stately Dallam Tower. Look right to see Milnthorpe
Bridge, an elegant single-span bridge, pleasingly reflected in the river. A delightful rural view is to be seen through its arch.

Go through another similar kissing gate onto a narrow road. Turn right and
stroll on to cross the busy B-road to Arnside. Pass through a small wooden gate
and continue beside the river to take another gate ahead.

Turn left and follow the river as it bears left here. Saunter on along the lovely
way, with the wide estuary stretching away to your right. Continue on to take a
reinforced rising path, on your left, that leads to the track bed of a dismantled

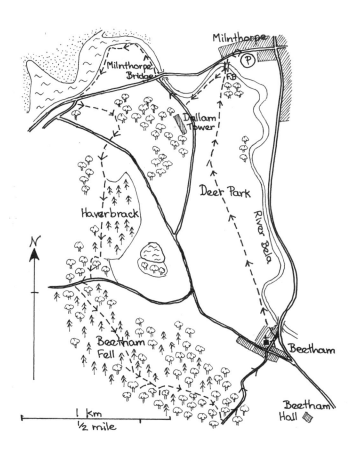

railway. Turn right and walk the tree-lined way to climb the next stile. Beyond carry on the narrow path, which brings you to a flight of steps to the road.

Cross the road with care into the start of a narrow road, which bears right and runs parallel to the B-road. Walk a few steps to take the two-armed sign-posted footpath on the left of this minor road. Take the path bearing left through woodland to a ladder stile. Beyond stride ahead, with a wall to your left, to go over two stiles on either side of a short access track, which leads into a pasture.

Beyond the second stile a waymark directs you right into more woodland. The next arrow points the way up a good path, at the edge of the trees, the way coming close to the high wall on your right. Continue to a stile, beyond which you cross a track and go through a kissing gate on the opposite side. Climb up-hill, with the wall to your left. Pause as you go to look back to see Whitbarrow Scar. Pause again on your ascent to look for a fine view of Milnthorpe tucked in a fold in the hills, with the Howgills stretching along the horizon beyond.

Jay

Continue climbing steadily to the boundary wall ahead. Here a kissing gate gives access to Haverbrack Wood and a signpost directing you right. The glorious track takes you on through limestone woodland, where jays call and where you might see a sparrow hawk flying low through the trees after prey. Look for spindle bushes, with bright magenta berries in autumn and, purging buckthorn, it too laden with masses of black fruit towards the end of the year.

At the three-armed signpost, turn right in the direction of Cockshot Lane, to carry on along a narrower track through the pleasing woodland. At a branching take the left fork and descend steadily to join a road. Turn right and walk on to take, on the left, a broad track, signposted Slackhead.

Eventually the track through the trees leads into a delightful clearing with a cairn, which supports an arrowed and named plate. Walk on in the direction of Bentham and go ahead through more limestone woodland to come to a T-junction of tracks. Ahead is a large, tall estate gate, slatted in wood and hung between iron posts. Here turn left and begin a gentle descent to another cairn with a direction plate on it. Bear right and go on along a wide track, through trees, with a fine limestone escarpment to your right.

Press on along the track to join the road at Slackhead. Turn left and stride the road, with care. Look right to see the remains of Beetham Hall, now a farm. It was originally built as a fortified manor house in 1340. Eleven generations of the de Beetham family lived in the dwelling. Continue steadily downhill to Beetham, enjoying the grand view into Yorkshire as you go. Continue past the Wheatsheaf Inn and go on to pass the church on your left. Just before you reach the A6, turn left into a narrow road, with the River Bela to your right.

Stroll on to a gap stile into Dallam Tower park. Climb steadily through an avenue of young trees to a stile. Beyond a stone slab takes you across a ha-ha (a deepish trench that acts as a fence, keeping the stock in or out, as desired, but not obstructing the view). Walk ahead over the delectable pasture. Look for the herd of fallow deer that are such a feature of the park.

Pass through the right end of a row of lofty horse chestnut and lime trees to follow a clearer track that leads to another cairn with a direction plate. Go on towards Milnthorpe to come to the stone bridge over the Bela. Cross and turn right to return to the car park or the village square for buses and toilets.

Walk 52: Arnside Knott

*Eaves Wood – Elmslack – Middlebarrow Plain – Arnside Tower – Arnside
Knott – Redhills Wood – Arnside Moss – Carr Bank – Black Dyke –
Railway Line – Middlebarrow Quarry – Far Waterslack – Eaves Wood*

Start/finish: Small easy-to-miss car park on the edge of Eaves Wood, Silverdale (GR
472759). It lies north-west of Leighton Moss visitor centre. Parts of Eaves Wood have
been a broad-leaved woodland continuously since the 1600s.

Type of walk: A pleasing 5½-mile walk through woodlands, over limestone and onto
a fine viewpoint. The paths are generally good and the gradient easy, even up onto
the Knott. One short section of footpath can be very muddy after rain, but it is possible
to walk Carr Bank Road, parallel with the path, and so remain mud-free.

Map: OS Outdoor Leisure 7 (new series).

Nearest town: Arnside.

Public transport: North Western trains; join walk at the Limestone Link footpath, inquiries 0345 484950. Stagecoach Cumberland Kendal-Arnside; some buses from
Lancaster call at Arnside, inquiries 01946 63222.

Refreshments: Arnside. None on-route, divert to Leighton Moss visitor centre on
your return.

Public toilets: Arnside.

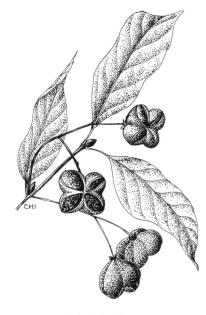

Spindle berries

Leave the back of the parking area by a
wide track into glorious ash, hazel and
oak woodland. Here in early autumn
you might spot the magenta berries of
the spindle tree, to the right of the
track. At the waymark, turn left to continue along the edge of the wood.
Through a gap in the trees you can see
the series of silvery limestone hills that
give Silverdale its name.

Follow the waymarks and, where
paths branch off, keep on the wide
track. Go on close beside a high limestone wall on the left. Ignore all right
and left turns and continue to join a
narrow road, lined with pretty cottages, at Elmslack.

Turn right and, when you can see
the woodstore of a house ahead, take
an unmarked narrow path, climbing
right into more woodland. Go through
a gap stile in the wall on the left. Take
the next gap stile, with a caravan site

screened by trees on the left. At the division of the track take the right branch
and, on joining a grassy trod, bear right again.

Carry on the lovely way to join a wide track and still go on right. Just before
you reach a T-junction of tracks, with a wall beyond, turn left to walk downhill to
a ladder stile to Arnside Tower. This is now a ruined shell. It was built for defence against pillaging Scots.

Arnside Tower

Beyond the stile, walk the good track to come to Arnside Tower farmhouse. Go
through the gate below the signpost and bear left along the access track.
Ahead is a grand view of the eroded side of the Knott, with scattered yew trees
valiantly holding back some of the scree.

Cross the Silverdale-Arnside road to go through a gate to join a public
bridleway. This takes you, left, through more lovely woodland, with pleasing ex-
posures of limestone. Pass through a gate and walk on. Three hundred metres
along go through another gate, set back on the right. This wide track climbs
gently uphill through a wonderland of scattered birch, beech, yew, juniper, oak
and Scots pine.

The seat at the top of the slope is just the place for your first break, with a
glorious view back down the slope and out over the sands of Morecambe Bay.
Turn right and continue on a wide terraced path (along which carriages con-
veyed much earlier tourists to the top of the Knott) to another seat from where
you have a fine view of the Lakeland fells and of Arnside viaduct.

Continue on the main track to come to a gate through the wall on your left.
Descend the grassy path over a pasture towards Redhills Wood on your right.
Three hundred metres before the corner of the pasture, go through the kissing
gate into trees. Walk ahead and go over a cross of tracks. When you have al-

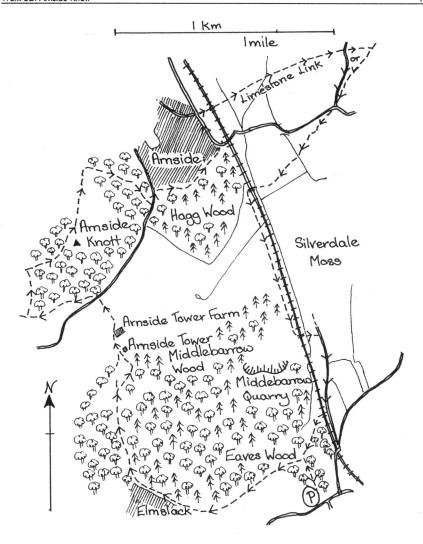

most reached the edge of the wood you meet a much wider track, where you turn right. Follow the clear way until it joins the main road, crossed earlier below the Knott.

Cross and turn left to walk beside the cemetery, on your right. Turn right into Spiny Lane, signposted "Footpath to Black Dyke". Stride ahead and, where the lane soon turns sharp left, walk ahead to take a narrow track between two dwellings – it is waymarked but the post is often obscured by vegetation. The next waymark directs you right to enter Hagg Wood.

Go down the clear rough path to join Black Dyke road. Cross and bear left to walk on to the signpost for the Limestone Link, directing you right along a track to the side of the gated railway line. (This is the point where rail travellers start the walk.) Cross the track with care and go on the fenced path across Arnside Moss.

At the signpost, ignore the left turn and go ahead over open pasture to a gap stile to a narrow road, Carr Bank Road, which you cross. Stroll ahead to take a stone step stile on the right, just before a gate. Pause on the top step to look back to see Hazelslack Tower. Turn right to walk a widish path through bushes that takes you to another step stile to the road. (If there has been much rain, it is better to turn right to walk Carr Bank Road, which runs parallel with the path.)

From the stile, or the end of the narrow road, turn right to take the sign-posted stile on the left. Strike half right to walk the pathless way to join a sturdy reinforced track, where you turn left. Stay on this until you reach a railway bridge, which you pass under, going through two gates. Beyond, turn left and continue beside the track. Look right for an imposing view of Arnside Tower.

Cross two footbridges, the second one taking you into Middlebarrow Wood. Suddenly, you come to Middlebarrow Quarry. (If it is working, you will want to hurry away from the noise.) Cross the railway track and walk on along the narrow road – with care because of the wagons carrying aggregate. Follow the road as it bears right and, after a further $\frac{3}{4}$ of a mile, take the signposted footpath, on the right, for Eaves Wood.

Go over the railway line again and walk ahead to pass through a gate. Bear left through the buildings of the charming Old Waterslack farm. Ignore the track going right, and go on the reinforced and then metalled way. Just beyond the last barn, where there are "no parking" signs, take the gap stile through the wall, on the right, into the wood.

Follow the path up the slope and continue where it bears left. Ignore the first path, which climbs a slope on the right. Continue on to follow the path and then climb the next slope right, to join the main track to the car park. Turn left and you are back.

Sigma Leisure Tea Shop Walks:

FIRST & BEST
IN THE LAKE DISTRICT!

TEA SHOP WALKS IN THE LAKE DISTRICT

Jean Patefield

This was the first-ever collection of Tea Shop Walks in the Lake District! Clear directions, fascinating background information and accurate maps ensure that with this book, you're sure of an excellent day in superb countryside. As a bonus, each walk has a tried and tested Lakeland tea shop that welcomes walkers – just imagine: an easy stroll with magnificent scenery followed by scones with strawberry jam and other delights! A leisurely introduction to the Lake District – and one that's just perfect for family walks. So good that it's now in its second edition! £6.95

MORE TEA SHOP WALKS IN THE LAKE DISTRICT

Norman & June Buckley

Norman and June Buckley have planned more leisurely rambles in this, the companion volume to our original tea shop book on the region. Crossing both the magnificent central regions and the lesser-known fringe areas, their 25, circular walks range from 2 to 9 miles and suit all ages and experience – perfect for family expeditions. As always, you are certain to be rewarded by a refreshing break in one of the carefully chosen tea shops along the way. Choose from tea rooms on a working farm, in a former Quaker meeting house or in the World of Beatrix Potter. "Clearly defined paths probe attractive countryside from Caldbeck Fells to Hampsfell" KESWICK REMINDER £6.95

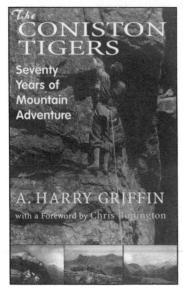